Liturgy Committee
BASICS

Thomas Baker and Frank Ferrone

Liturgy Committee
BASICS

A No-nonsense Guide

The Pastoral Press
Washington, D.C.

ISBN: 0-912405-11-2

The Pastoral Press
225 Sheridan Street, NW
Washington, D.C. 20011
(202) 723-5800

The Pastoral Press is the publications division of the National Association of Pastoral Musicians, a membership organization of musicians and clergy dedicated to fostering the art of musical liturgy.

Printed in the United States of America

CONTENTS

Preface | 1

CHAPTER ONE
The Problem and Some Solutions | 4

CHAPTER TWO
Politics | 22

CHAPTER THREE
Membership | 36

CHAPTER FOUR
Leadership | 52

CHAPTER FIVE
The Agenda | 66

CHAPTER SIX
How to Talk about Liturgy | 78

Appendix | 100

PREFACE

Writing this book was a lot of fun. After years of Sunday evening quarterbacking, it pleases us to think that maybe some of the headaches we've encountered may be learned from. The Pastoral Press and Dan Connors especially have been patient, encouraging and helpful. They also have been a source of a few good laughs (and a couple of cheesesteaks).

Thanks go to The Rev. Charles B. Weiser of Princeton University's Aquinas Institute for implanting the belief at an impressionable (if not early) age that liturgy committees really ought to exist. We also owe a debt to Georgetown University's campus ministry and especially The Rev. Larry Madden, S.J., Ed Walker, and Elaine Rendler. They provided many of the positive insights that went into this book. We won't tell you who provided the bad examples.

Finally, we know this book owes its existence to our wives, Sue McSorley and Mimi Mahon. Their goading made it all possible.

The
Problem
and Some
Solutions

It's probably not a good idea to begin by mangling a great opening by Tolstoy, but the fact remains: Most good liturgy committees can be vastly different in how they operate, while the bad ones all seem to be bad in the same ways.

Just as they have in many other parts of American life, regional differences and oddball uniqueness seem to have disappeared when it comes to liturgy committees. In big parishes and small, rural and urban, "active" and "inactive," the liturgy committee meeting is for some reason a sitting duck for sublimated hostility, inaction, and sheer boredom. For anyone who's wound up attending a liturgy committee meeting they'd like to forget, the following all-too-true examples will sound familiar.

• A meeting to "plan Advent and Christmas" becomes an extended debate on Christmas decorations. Did we have enough trees last year? Can't we light the manger scene outside? Who'll hang the wreaths? Elapsed time: 1 hr. 45 min. Actual planning: 0.

• A meeting to evaluate the year's progress suddenly becomes an evaluation of the schedule. Can we move the 10:15 to 10:30 so we can clear away the mess after the 9:15? No, we had the 10:15 at 10:30 five years ago and nobody came. Well, we could move the 9:15 to 9:00, and then we could take the...no, no, we can't move the 9:15. The 9:15?? Don't you know who goes to that? Bruised egos: 3. Actual planning: 0.

• The first item on a carefully typed agenda, deciding the date and time for the next meeting, becomes a power struggle. Well, I'm sorry, but Tuesday night is my opera night this year, and of course Father Porter can only make it on Mondays, so Mondays it will have to be. Well, who said *Father Porter* had to be here for us to have a meeting? Mondays is the one night *I* can't make it! Elapsed time on insignificant item: 45 mins. Long-standing conflicts papered over: 2. Actual planning: 0.

• A highly paid music director is requested to present his music selections for Palm Sunday to the parish committee for review—song by song. Oh, I just can't *imagine* Palm Sunday without "O Sacred Head Surrounded"—can we have it somewhere, as a solo? And I know just the person to sing it! Grey hairs for music director: Untold. Actual planning: 0.

We could go on and on—just the way many liturgy

committee meetings do. In one parish you see detailed ''planning'' being done by people who don't even attend the liturgy in question, and music being selected by non-musicians. In another you find uncomfortable boredom, as people of good will try to plan liturgies with no concept of what there is to plan. You can find elaborate plans for specific liturgies or for entire seasons—yet with no structured forum for evaluation after it's over. You can find lots of argument about liturgy that boils down to criticism of what someone else finds helpful.

Above all, there are meetings—usually long ones. And they're long for a reason: Starved for a real sense of what to do, or paralyzed by members with plenty to defend but not much to offer, liturgy committees will tend to focus on the safe, the manageable—the trivial.

Sometimes all this trivia hides deep ideological conflicts. Sometimes it's a conscious direction provided by an insecure staff. Sometimes, it's simply not having an answer to this question: What are we all doing here?

WHY BOTHER?

Before you start a liturgy committee in your parish, or before you join one, see if you can articulate exactly *why* you're doing it. Examining and expressing your reasons up front will prevent a lot of trouble down the line.

The official reason (see ''Upon This Rock,'' right) for liturgy committees is simple. Liturgy articulates and supports the faith of the community, and that means the community gets involved.

That means: The community *must* be represented in the planning and evaluation of its liturgies. It is crucial for the clergy and professional staff of the parish to be both encouraged and supervised by a wide variety of community members. It is the community's job to make sure that the needs of its members—and there will be a great variety of needs, changing constantly—are reflected in its liturgical life.

But it doesn't mean: That liturgy is supposed to be a democracy, or that a community's liturgies are planned by majority votes on individual decisions. It doesn't mean that the parish avoids using the best people it can find to be its presiders and professional liturgists, and it doesn't mean that

continued

Upon This Rock

While the term ''liturgy committee'' has a peculiarly American ring, its existence is in fact sanctioned—however weakly—in the *General Instruction of the Roman Missal,* Rome's manual on how to celebrate the eucharist.

> *All concerned* [italics ours] should work together in the effective preparation of each liturgical celebration as to its rites, pastoral aspects, and music. (Section 73)

When you read through the *General Instruction* in its entirety, however, do not be surprised to find a variety of passages which might seem to deemphasize such participation. For example:

> Thus in carrying out this [liturgical] function, all, whether ministers or laypersons, should do all and only those parts that belong to them... (Section 58)

What parts ''belong to them,'' of course, will depend on your point of view.

Somewhat more inspiring (and less ambiguous) is this passage from the American bishops' 1972 (revised 1983) *Music in Catholic Worship:*

> The planning team or committee is headed by the priest (celebrant and homilist) for no congregation can experience the richness of a unified celebration if that unity is not grasped by the one who presides, as well as by those who have special roles. The planning group should include those with the knowledge and artistic skills needed in celebration: men and women trained in music, poetry, and art, and familiar with current resources in this area; men and women sensitive also to the present-day thirst of so many for the riches of scripture, theology, and prayer. It is always good to include some members of the congregation who have not taken special roles in the

celebrations so that honest evaluations can be made. (Section 12)

Let's leave aside for the moment the apparent assumption that priests need to be in charge in order to grasp things (we'll touch on this in Chapter Three). The rest of that paragraph—with its emphasis on sensitivity to liturgical skills as well as liturgical rules, and its recognition of the need for "honest evaluations"—is a wonderfully concise summary of what liturgy committees are about.

You can find these and other important liturgical documents listed in the Appendix.

you shouldn't leave these people alone to do their jobs. It doesn't mean that individuals with strong feelings can run roughshod over an established community, or prevent the establishment of a new liturgy if they find it not to their taste. And above all, what it doesn't mean is that the liturgy should *look* like it was done by a committee: slow, bland, uncertain, and full of careful compromises.

Does all this sound contradictory? Perhaps. Liturgy committees are unique in most people's experience of organizational life.

We all know about autocracy, dictatorship, collaboration, democracy, teams—we know how these things work, and how we're supposed to behave when we're involved in one of them. But liturgy committees don't really fit into any of these categories very neatly. Suddenly we need to be both democratic and undemocratic. We are eager for independent, expert help but ultimately its employer. We are uneducated in music and theater, but are asked to evaluate their effect on the liturgy. We respond emotionally to an event but are asked occasionally to respect the emotional reactions of others. We may be accustomed to being uncritical of the church but now must deal with what may be the faults of its clergy.

These are uncharted waters. And most liturgy committees are, to put it mildly, at sea.

Yet all is not lost. The problem here is not the concept. The problem is that management science, or canon law, or whatever, has not yet given the liturgy committee what any organization needs to survive: A mission. For a company, that mission is profits, or outstanding computers. For a college, the mission is education, or football. The liturgical planning process and those involved in it need a goal, a yardstick like these. A few sentences to come back to when no one quite knows what to do next.

And for liturgy committee members too, there are only a few important things missing: A job description. A way of knowing what you're there for. A way of talking about liturgy.

In the remainder of this book we hope to help you a little with these problems. Let's begin with four simple statements about what liturgy committees do.

ONE

First, let's take a close look at the word most used in the area of liturgy committees: planning. Ask anyone what liturgy committees are supposed to do—ask the chairperson of your committee. They'll answer: We're supposed to plan liturgies.

Wrong.

If we communicate one concept in this book, it should be this: The liturgy committee represents the consensus of the community in matters relating to its liturgical life. If some of its members are involved in "planning" a particular liturgy, that's all for the good. But the liturgy committee model that pictures a group—usually a rather miscellaneous one—reviewing the details week by week on a variety of liturgies has a serious and limiting flaw in its definition of liturgy.

A liturgy is more than a multiple-choice problem—a string of questions with a limited number of answers to each part, where the planning process consists of plugging in one of the answers, perhaps even by vote. It is, perhaps, this model of planning that yields the frozen liturgy, one which remains the same not because it doesn't need change but because the larger questions of its effectiveness are so hard to reduce to a bunch of composite parts to be voted up or down. A liturgy is far more a work of art than a quiz, and composing it should be left to the artists: your presider, your musicians, your director of liturgy, your people with talent.

Do you have poor presiders and musicians? As a liturgy committee you are supposed to do something about it, and we'll get to that later. For now let's articulate the first rule of liturgy committees:

> **1. Liturgical planning (the actual selection of music, the work on the homily, the writing of the prayers, and the orchestration of all the other variables that make up a liturgy) should be left to the people you choose as your experts, preferably as small and as talented a group as possible. Empower them and leave them alone.**

On one level, this makes sense simply from an organizational point of view—you won't get good people, or

This supremely important principle of social philosophy, one which cannot be set aside or altered, remains firm and unshaken: Just as it is wrong to withdraw from the individual and commit to the community at large what private enterprise and endeavor can accomplish, so it is likewise unjust and a gravely harmful disturbance of right order to turn over to a greater society of higher rank functions and services which can be performed by lesser bodies on a lower plane. For a social undertaking of any sort, by its very nature, ought to aid the members of the body social, but never to destroy and absorb them.[1]

When Pius XI set forth this principle of "subsidiarity," he gave the church a rule that it has since applied in a variety of analyses, from development economics to the theory of private property. It has, you may have noticed, been somewhat less successful in applying it to the Roman church itself.[2]

No matter. Subsidiarity is not just a theory that tries to preserve human dignity, but a recognition of some basic propensities of human nature: People work better and get more out of things when they have (or even *think* they have) autonomy over the concerns that they think they are better qualified to judge than anyone else. If you are prepared to admit that the principle is a valid one—*and if* you are willing to go so far as to say that liturgy is in any sense a "social undertaking"—then subsidiarity suggests some guidelines for liturgy committees that are both practical and moral.

1. Don't impose uniformity where there doesn't need to be any.
2. Don't waste your time on small matters someone else could be deciding.
3. Your committee exists to help liturgies, not be in charge of them.

continued

keep them very long, or get very much work out of them, if you don't leave them alone to do what they've been trained (we hope) to do well. But it doesn't mean that you, as a liturgy committee, are supposed to leave them *completely* alone. You are there to evaluate their performance. If they're doing a bad job, or violating the rules you established, or not working out with the communities they've been assigned to, make it your business to do something about it. By saying that you should leave your experts alone, we're not suggesting a return to the days of let-Father-do-it. Far from it. A combination of independence and supervision will put far greater demands on Father's competence than it may have ever had before.

TWO

It's impossible to imagine how many liturgy committee members wind up sitting in judgment on the value or competence of a liturgy or liturgist they've neither seen nor heard. It is also not unusual to see—as we did in the examples earlier—a group of people far too involved in an issue not affecting the liturgical life of the liturgy they regularly attend.

Why is this so bad? For several reasons: It fosters complacency. Decisions get made on hearsay. The rights of communities can be violated. And again, it's a simple case of good management: You rarely bring in a bunch of people who aren't familiar with a situation and ask them to make a decision about its life or death.

The principle involved here is not a new one. Pius XI—yes, Pius XI—articulated it quite well (see "Small Is Still Beautiful," left) in his principle of subsidiarity: Work should be done by the smallest group competent to do it. The implication is clear, and that introduces our second principle:

2. Planning for a liturgy should be done only by people who are members of the community that celebrates that liturgy. The task of evaluating that liturgy is also, first and foremost, theirs.

Now on the surface this might seem to leave nothing left over for the parish liturgy committee to do, but nothing could be further from the truth. The parish committee's job is a vastly wide-ranging one, far wider than a typical parish meeting would lead you to believe. There are plenty of agenda items left, and we'll be dealing with them as we go on.

A more telling criticism of this second principle is that it seems to leave lots of liturgies with no one to take care of them. After all, how many liturgies are there in your parish with an identifiable, regular group of people who are willing to take charge?

Not many, right? That's a problem—probably one of the most difficult with which we'll deal in this book. Because we're proposing that each liturgy needs just such a group—a presider, musicians, and committed and talented community members—to be a terrific liturgy. It needs people who, week by week, work to plan that liturgy and evaluate it after it's over. Oh yes, it can lack such a group and be just fine. But remarkable? A liturgy you won't want to miss, that you would want to bring your friends to, that will build a community? We think it's unlikely, and we hope to convince you of that. And if you think liturgies like that aren't what you're after, perhaps you should think twice about being on a liturgy committee, because liturgies like that are what committees are supposed to make possible.

THREE

If "planning" is the most *over*used word in the liturgical life of most parishes, then "evaluation" is the most *under*used. Because by evaluation we're not talking about a quick post mortem, a catalog of errors, a list of who did what wrong. We're talking about the whole reason to put the community's resources into the liturgy at all: Did our work make a difference? Did we accomplish what we really set out to do? What was the liturgy *like*?

Liturgy committees can go for years without ever addressing these questions, yet they should be at the top of every agenda at every meeting. To plan a liturgy means that you have a result in mind; to evaluate a liturgy means to measure against that goal.

> **3. No liturgical planning process—for a particular weekly liturgy, a special occasion, or a parish's liturgical life as a whole—is complete without a genuine evaluation.**

1. From *Quadragesimo Anno* (1931). Quoted in *The Gospel of Peace and Justice*, ed. Joseph Gremillion (Maryknoll: Orbis, 1977), p. 322.

2. "Subsidiarity began to wane in the Church," writes who else but Andrew M. Greeley, "when the cable and steamship reinforced the autocratic propensities of the Renaissance papacy" (in *No Bigger Than Necessary* [New York: Meridian, 1977], p. 14).

Now we're not suggesting that each liturgy, each week, has to be followed by a session of agonizing reappraisal. But we are saying that part of every parish's liturgical structure has to be evaluations—of those charged with celebrating the liturgies, of the direction of a particular liturgy, of the parish as a whole.

Why don't people evaluate? The harsh answer would be that they don't want to *be* evaluated or have a comfortable tradition scrutinized, or because clergy or staff resist the very concept. More common, however, is probably the simplest answer of all—they don't know what they were really trying to "do" in the first place. The result? What passes for evaluation at those meetings that make an attempt to deal with it. I liked it. Period. I didn't like it. Period.

Evaluating, in a way, is a lot harder than planning, but that could only be because planning *seems* so much easier after you begin to evaluate regularly. Setting up a process of evaluation forces you to articulate what you want in the first place. And when you know what your overall yardstick will be, that makes it easier to make your more detailed decisions about what will go on at your liturgy—just as an outline for a book (articulating what you want) makes the actual writing (planning and execution) a whole lot easier. The things you do in liturgy should be done for a reason, and with a goal in mind; evaluation forces you to face up to this fact, and to make choices based on *the result you want* and not on repeating the only things you happen to know. Think of evaluating not so much as a report card on a liturgy but as a way of forcing yourself to set goals for a liturgy, and of putting your own reactions—even emotional ones—into words.

FOUR Unfortunately,
adhering to the first three of our principles requires a little bureaucracy.

Each liturgy, as we have said, requires a group to meet regularly and map out its general direction, give guidance to its team of experts, and evaluate that liturgy regularly. "Above" that group, there should be a parish committee—and their agenda is the liturgical life of the parish as a whole.

What we have here, ideally, is a two-tiered structure: A liturgy committee for each liturgy in the parish (for the sake of convenience, from here on we'll call these the planning groups), and a liturgy committee for the parish. We'll deal with their interrelationship later. For now, let's propose our fourth and final rule:

> **4. The parish committee's job is not to plan liturgies, but to set goals, direction, and standards for the overall liturgical life and activities of the parish. One of these goals should be creating and encouraging regular planning groups for each parish liturgy. It should work with these groups but leave them alone except for periodic evaluation.**

Thank you, Pius XI: Big groups decide questions that need the big group. Little groups should take care of themselves.

What does the *parish committee* do? It talks about the liturgies the parish has—largely in terms of how well the planning groups are functioning. If a liturgy lacks committed individuals to care for it, the parish committee discusses the problem. It tries to find (and fund) the resources each group needs. It regularly attends and thinks about each liturgy the parish has (this alone would be revolutionary for most liturgy committees). It has a variety of very big issues to discuss:

- Is the overall liturgical profile of the parish varied enough? Of high enough quality?
- What would be the response of a person walking in off the street to liturgy X, or Y, or Z? What are *our* responses?
- What are the alternatives to our current lineup of liturgies?
- Will particular seasons or feasts affect *all* our parish's liturgies? In what ways?
- Are there liturgies that are not supporting a community, serving no purpose?
- Is our money being spent in the best possible way? Are we devoting enough of the parish's resources to liturgy?
- Is there criticism that needs to be given to the parish staff? To lectors? To ushers?

In short, the constant questions for parish committees: Are our liturgies good enough? What can we do better?

These are tough questions—questions most well-meaning parishioners will feel themselves unequipped to discuss. We hope to show them that they're wrong—that all they need are common sense, a little practice in articulating reactions and emotions, and a little exposure to good, affecting liturgy.

What does a *planning group* do? It meets, ideally weekly, to discuss the previous Sunday's liturgy, both in terms of the success or failure of particular experiments and in terms of the general effectiveness of the liturgy. It will discuss future liturgies and liturgical seasons—both the established readings and traditions and whatever ideas and previous experiences the group's members bring to the meeting. It will mull over ideas, visual images, moods, music that best articulate that season or liturgy. And it will then let its own team of "experts"—presider, musicians, writers, artists, lectors, whomever—work on the areas delegated to them. Periodically, the group will undertake some evaluation of its supply of experts, and of the direction of the liturgy as a whole.

It's a wonderful system—in theory. Now all you need are the right people.

FINDING THE RIGHT PEOPLE

Stop right there, you may say. That's the whole problem. I can't get anyone to join the committee. Or the people I've got on it don't want to belong to it, don't have any ideas, or have nothing but a laundry list of things they *don't* want. Besides—why should anyone join my committee?

Good liturgy committee members will join for one reason only: Because you've got a well-run group, a group that knows what it's supposed to do, does it expeditiously, and has fun doing it.

How many people join (or get conned into joining) a group just because they feel like they should? Or because they systematically join every parish organization on a rotating basis? Or—to be frank—because they've got nothing better to do?

We're going to be extremely harsh, and tell you that you don't want these people—at least, not on these terms. The people who should be on parish liturgy committees are articulate and interested. That means they're probably busy. They don't have time for groups that sit around wasting it.

They want to know exactly what you want them to do.

Whether you're starting a new committee, recruiting new members for an old one, or cleaning house in a committee with problems, you owe it to everyone to produce what everyone with a job to do deserves: a job description. The job you want done, what you expect of them, how much of their time and energy it will all take. Yes, tell them how much it will mean to the community, and how much they stand to learn. But above all, give them a clear sense of what the committee is for, and what its members are for.

Ask some average parishioners what they think they would have to know to join the liturgy committee. Those who don't think that Latin is a prerequisite would probably guess that some expertise in the liturgical documents and rubrics would be. Go one step further and ask them what they think happens at a typical liturgy meeting, and you'll probably get a puzzled silence. Whatever they're picturing in their minds, it probably doesn't look like fun.

They would probably be surprised to hear that the primary prerequisite for membership should be the ability to *talk*.

You may have plenty of talk already, and you may be sick of it. But what you need is *real* talk about liturgy—reactions to liturgy, preferably emotional yet experienced reactions. You need talk that tries to figure out what *caused* these reactions. Contrast that with most "talk" you hear at liturgy meetings: "I hate things like that." "Was that legal?" "That was just plain *old*."

You can do a lot to nip this kind of talk right in the bud. Create a job description for your liturgy committee members, and (as we'll discuss in Chapter Three) create an actual admissions process that screens out people who just don't fit the bill. Cruel? Perhaps—but not any more cruel than some of the meetings we described at the beginning of this chapter.

For now consider the following criteria for membership on any liturgy committee, either at the parish level or for an individual liturgy. Use some or all of them, but do use them—adapt them and publish them in the bulletin each fall and spring, hand them out to prospective members. You'll find that such a process turns off some of those who don't want to do what you're describing—and intrigues those who might not otherwise come forward.

A JOB DESCRIPTION

1.● You must be interested in attending liturgies.

This doesn't mean studying them academically—although someone with a thorough knowledge of the Coptic night office, or some such, is a terrific resource as well as good for laughs. It also doesn't mean a *proprietary* interest in liturgy—people with a style or a particular liturgy that (so they think) is indispensable to the life of the church. You'll find a lot of these people on liturgy committees—and in the clergy and as professional musicians. You'll need plenty of people with a *real* interest to counteract them.

What we mean by "interested in liturgy" is more a case of someone—at one time or another—having been profoundly affected by liturgy. It may only have been a single liturgy in one time and place, or a regular community that someone found memorable and sustaining. But that experience gave them a certain curiosity about how liturgy works—about why some liturgies produce these profound feelings of presence and celebration, and others don't even rate the word boring. Most such people are always looking for another liturgy or community that can recreate that powerful experience from their past. If they can distance themselves from that past experience to some extent—that is, if they can realize that the point is not to recreate a very likely un-recreatable experience, but to see what in that experience was so memorable—these are the ideal people to work on liturgy.

You'll find plenty of people in your search who think that they "like" liturgy. That they "love the mass." That they feel called upon to learn about this great repository of tradition. That the mass is the primary focus of their spiritual lives. These are all admirable things, but in the search for a liturgy committee they are red flags. Find people who know what they're looking for but haven't found it yet, not people who'll take anything as long as it's what they're familiar with. You'll probably find yourself with a smaller number of committee members but far better off in both ideas and efficiency.

2.
You are willing to serve—not pay lip service to—the parish as a whole.

Using our first criterion alone, you'll find people with a point of view. But a point of view is not the same thing as a set of pet peeves.

It's easy to find people who have an allegiance to a particular liturgy, or at least to a liturgical style with which they are comfortable. But people who *genuinely* feel that the parish ought to reflect a variety of needs are another story.

People who hate organ music usually hate it even when they're not hearing it—not only don't they want it at the liturgy they go to, they secretly don't want it even at the other parish liturgies. They'll fight to keep the organist from getting a raise, and God forbid they should actually *go* to the organ mass and try to see what everyone likes so much, or whether there is anything that can be said in its favor.

Expand this question still further—can you find people who would be willing to venture inside a *Protestant* church? Perhaps to see whether it really is irresistible when a big Lutheran congregation (or even a small one) shakes the roof with a hymn? Or whether the standards of preaching really are higher at the Episcopal cathedral? You need people who realize that what goes on inside these other buildings is liturgy, too.

Lots of people think they're open-minded. But remember—your committee is going to ask these people to go to these other liturgies, and to go without preconceived notions. Not that we think everyone ought to find every liturgy equally conducive—but we do think that good liturgy and bad liturgy happen in every style and every denomination, and you need people who at least have the potential of distinguishing the issue of quality from the issue of what they personally prefer.

You'll also find plenty of people who think they have their finger on the pulse of the parish—they usually play the role of the Great Protector. On any given decision or evaluation, they are sure to identify individuals, or even whole communities, who will be irreparably damaged by headlong and foolish change. This tendency to trot out a nonexistent Silent Liturgical Majority is a common one, and can easily result in inconclusive knife-throwing in meetings. Again, try to minimize this during your recruitment process, and find a balance among the strengths and weaknesses of your initial group—*and* find a chairperson who knows enough to distinguish genuine concern from an obvious ploy.

3.

You must be able to talk.

Again, let's define "talk" as more than opinions. Talk is evaluating a liturgy's quality: articulating your reactions in terms of the specific actions that caused the reactions.

This doesn't have to be—and shouldn't be—overly touchy-feely. You don't have to go into the spiritual experiences you had during the communion meditation, particularly if you tend to have them regularly. But you should be able to answer a few basic questions about any liturgy you attend:

- What caused your reactions, positive or negative?
- Was there an overall problem, or were there just a few things wrong?
- What was good, and what wasn't?
- Can you imagine a group of people finding this liturgy rewarding? Why? For *good* reasons?
- Was it a good liturgy, even if it wasn't one you'd attend? What would you change about it?

These are the kinds of questions your committee ought to be addressing, and in a civilized manner. If you think you've got someone who's not willing to go on these little liturgical field trips, wait for someone who is.

One final point: Don't think that by prescribing people who can talk that we want you to wind up with meeting hogs or showoffs, people with a mouthful on any subject. If this happens, we hope you have a chairperson who knows how and when to clamp down on your more garrulous members.

4.

You must be willing to fight for what you need.

Realistically, it won't be unusual for a committee or a planning group to need to go through a good bit of conflict to get what it deserves. Liturgies deserve good presiders, good homilies, good music, and money to pay for them. You may find you have none of the above.

Often of course, the situation is irreparable. Your parish may not have nearly enough money even for lights and heat, or there may not be any priests in the area who would agree to visit your parish and preach or preside occasionally. But more often than not there is simply a long fight of some sort to be waged—with the parish council, with the pastor, with the music director. How much your committee has to say about such matters depends a great deal on the official role that has been established for it (see the next chapter). But whatever the case, the committee has a duty to place possibly sensitive issues on the agenda regularly. Find people who are willing to deal with them—directly but constructively.

5. ● You should not be bulldozeable by authorities.

The fact that your Ph.D. music director digs up a Bach cantata written to go with the very readings you have this Sunday doesn't make it an effective choice. You need people who aren't embarrassed to say so. Some ancient Christian practices have fallen into disuse because they were not helpful to the community; having a historian who can recall them verbatim may not be the shot in the arm your liturgy needs. Find people who are willing to listen, but who are willing on occasion to tell the emperor he has no clothes.

6. ● You must be willing to celebrate.

Here's the real shocker—it is sad to see how few people *enjoy* going about the work of liturgical planning.

In the first place, your meetings ought to be fun just so people stick with the group. If your committee is not providing its members with a certain level of friendship, satisfaction and laughs, you'll quickly find yourself with the members who simply have nothing better to do. You'll also discover that people who are uncomfortable together in an informal setting don't get very much good work done together either—and that tense or boring meetings translate into tense or boring liturgy.

Second, no one seems to realize that liturgy has tremendous opportunities for fun. Oh, not just making fun

17

of bad presiders and homilists, although that's definitely good for an occasional impersonation contest. The process of liturgical planning is very close to that of putting on a show—and people who put on shows usually have a keen sense of how funny it is when the carefully prepared goes awry, when a predictable personality suddenly begins his usual routine, when reality and real people make a surprising intrusion into a supposedly exalted activity. They also know the release of tension and the rush of satisfaction after a good production does exactly what it was supposed to do.

' We hope you at least have one person on your committee who can play the role of court jester. As for everyone else, make sure they're not horrified by the idea of laughing (after the fact) at what went wrong on Good Friday. Watch out for the people who just sit there quietly when everyone else seems to be having a good time.

7.
You must value liturgy as perhaps the most crucial service provided by your community.

We won't enter into the debate on whether a vital liturgical life flows from the personal commitment and political engagement of its members, or whether it's good liturgy that stops people in their tracks and urges them to conversion and service. (Is it possible both statements are true?) Let's just say the following: The liturgy, Sunday liturgy, is the most direct experience of church or community most Catholics in this country have. Each week, you as a community have one chance to reach, somehow, both those people who for some reason come to one of your liturgies every week and those who just happen to wander in. If not the most significant opportunity for ministry you are faced with each week, it is certainly the most obvious.

Liturgy is the activity most people identify with the word "church" for most of their lives ("I'm going to church now."). We won't bother you with the numbers on who goes and who doesn't. Just think about it this way. The people who *are* there are there because they're looking for something: Are you giving them everything you can? The people who *aren't* there are staying away because there's something they want to avoid, or because they want something they haven't found yet: What is it?

In your search for committee members, you don't have to find people who are interested in proselytizing, who want to run up to everyone after mass, shake their hands, and ask them how their spiritual lives are. But you *do* want people who regard liturgy as more than something they do for themselves—who know that in addition it is something we build to reach out to others.

How many of these people should you get? Who will choose them? How will you get things done? In the next chapter we begin to address these harsher realities.

Politics

Eugene Kennedy has called passive-aggressive behavior "the common cold of the emotions." While we are not psychologists by any stretch of the imagination, it doesn't take much experience working in church settings to see that worship somehow turns this common cold into an epidemic. It may be useful or consoling for you to be able to spot it.

What is it? Merely a way of acting out anger without acting angry. Many people—particularly those in church careers, but even regular laypeople in a church setting—subconsciously feel that really being mad or defensive just isn't appropriate, or doesn't fit in well with what they think they should be acting like. Inside, however, they're still mad and defensive—but they act it out quietly, innocently, passively.

"Passive-aggressives hurt people, not by doing things, but by failing to do them"—if any of these symptoms appear on a regular basis, you may be dealing with a passive-aggressive. Maybe you'll have someone fail to show up for an important planning session; that's a good way to put a stop to things without doing something overtly hostile. Or, perhaps you'll get a seemingly indifferent presider to agree to a particular change in the liturgy; during the liturgy itself, he will somehow manage to omit the change in question. Later he may deny any wrongdoing and say that he just goofed up, and in fact he may not be aware that he blocked your change (which he wasn't wild about) by playing dumb.

In other words, non-passive-aggressives say "No." Passive-aggressives say, "I forgot."

Quotations from Eugene Kennedy, *On Becoming a Counselor* (Seabury: New York, 1977), p. 21.

Now comes the first obstacle that stands in the way of any group attempting to organize itself and accomplish a goal. It's an obstacle that you'll run into whether you're a well-meaning pastor starting a new committee from scratch or a put-upon chairperson trying to get a bad situation moving again. The obstacle is politics. "Politics" encapsulates some nasty but basic questions: Who's got the power? Who can make the decisions that will affect our parish's liturgies? Who hires and fires? Who controls the money?

WHY POLITICS MATTERS

It's probably a fair statement that most liturgy committees have never addressed these issues formally. Yet they are at the heart of why most liturgy committees degenerate so easily into ineffectiveness and stagnancy.

What's going on in the terrible meeting examples we enumerated at the beginning of Chapter One? In most of them, a struggle for power. People discuss foolishly irrelevant topics, to some extent because those are the only topics they feel themselves empowered to discuss. People attempt agonizing appraisals of individual songs and prayers, largely in a passive-aggressive attempt to exert control by dithering someone into submission. (See "I Forgot...," left.) Severe criticism of liturgies takes the form of sneak attacks or sniping, often because the committee's evaluative role has not been clearly established.

You won't get the right people to join your committee, and you certainly won't have good liturgies, until you figure out why you're meeting and what you have the power to do. Most committees now in existence probably have an inflated notion of what they're entitled to do *and* what they're not—and in both cases, they're wrong.

You *should*, for example, be entitled to a voice in the way money is spent, in the assignment of presiders, in the hiring of staff, and in the general spirit of the parish's liturgical activities. In most cases, committees are not concerned—or permitted to be concerned—with these questions. On the other hand, you *shouldn't* be permitted to mess around with music selections, with homilies, or with the work of your professional staff; you shouldn't be spending inordinate amounts of time on the schedule, the flower arrangements, or the banners. Most of these aren't off limits because they're too important—they're not important *enough*. In the battle for good liturgy, they are insignificant targets that only seem important because the big problems are so hard to address.

Your liturgy committee has an enormous territory to cover, and a huge number of privileges to protect and defend. Your only hope is to articulate this territory up front—by writing a document that says what your committee is for, what it can do and what it can't.

If this sounds unnecessary, think again. Right now you may have a carefully worked out web of unspoken understandings and uncomfortable compromises. That may be all right for now, but the next big conflict may result in a surprising neglect of your gentlemen's agreement. And will your set-up survive a change in pastors? Of parish staff? Of committee leadership?

No, when the chips are down you'll wish you had something that says exactly where you stand. Your parish needs a task force to write such a document and to set up a system for its approval, modification and enforcement.

WORTH THE PAPER IT'S PRINTED ON?

Most parishes, as we've said, don't have such a document. And even if you write one, you'll have to realize that if push comes to shove it's going to look less like a charter and a lot more like a piece of paper.

Face it: Most parishes don't even have effective parish councils, much less a council whose decisions are to any degree binding on a pastor or bishop who chooses to ignore them. Take a look at the "constitution" of any parish that has been thoughtful or realistic enough to provide a firm foundation for its parish-council system. You'll more than likely find a sentence in there somewhere which boils down to the following: Parish councils are great, but they are only advisory. They can inform the pastor of their opinions. He can take their opinion or leave it, and if he decides to leave it—well, there's not very much they can do about it, other than resign, stop giving money, or make some other sort of public stink. None of these will be very effective in changing the situation.

What's true for parish councils is just as true for liturgy committees: You are very unlikely to work out a structure which gives your committee a role that is, ultimately, anything more than strictly advisory. In most dioceses, parish groups exist at the pleasure of the pastor. His decisions in the parish are binding, and he is encouraged but not by any means required (except in the case of parish finances) to seek counsel from the laity or his staff.

That's the bad news. If you are in a parish that doesn't want a liturgy committee, or where the depressing quality of the liturgies is directly traceable to the personality problems or insensitivity of the pastor, you are in a tough spot. You have two choices. You can, of course, do some serious parish shopping. Or you can tough it out and spend a great deal of time improving things where you can. Sad to say, many American Catholics will find themselves in this bind. If you are, for whatever reason, tied to a parish like this, we hope you will still find the rest of this book useful, as you attempt to find ways to improve your parish's liturgies without treading on any of the large number of land mines your pastor has buried for you. Please persevere.

But let's hope you have a pastor who is at least interested in forming a liturgy committee and hearing what it has to say. You may not improve his style as a homilist—but you may be able to mitigate it by convincing him to bring in other presiders occasionally. You may not get the ultimate say in who gets hired as music director—but you may be included somewhere strategic enough in the interviewing process to eliminate the clearly undesirable candidates.

But you will accomplish these things only if your role—whatever it is—has been clearly defined from the outset. Your greatest victories will be won not by blazing a trail through new territory in sensitive situations everyone finds threatening, but by routinely exercising influence in a framework which has come to be accepted as the norm. First lay out a system which calls for your participation; that system will work for you far better than a setting where your role needs to be re-debated whenever a tough decision comes up.

PRODUCING A DOCUMENT

We hope this book encourages your parish to produce a charter for your liturgy committee—and in a way, it doesn't matter exactly what sort of document you write.

What you come up with does not have to be a once-and-for-all Magna Carta. In some cases, it may be something the pastor works out privately with his liturgy committee members, or even with the committee chairperson alone over a few dinners out. The forum for arriving at such a document will be decided by the history and personalities of your parish. Its legitimacy will be determined only by how willing those concerned with the project are to accept it, not by how well it conforms to any theory of parish government. Democracy need not be your model for ratification—the process itself is far less important than how people feel about what the document says, and how good a system you have built in for changing the document later.

If you find yourself in the position of commissioning or working on such a document, you will find the field wide open. You can define the liturgical responsibilities of your committee, your music director, your staff, or your pastor in any way that the parties involved see fit to do so. Your charter does not need to be some outrageous bill of rights for the laity. But neither should it be an embarrassingly bland theory of parish and community that fails to deal with the very practical problems you'll be dealing with.

In short, be realistic, and write a document you'll actually use. Keep in mind that you'll need to think about the trouble spots and grey areas that your committee's deliberations are sure to lead you into. You may decide to write an expressly temporary document and use it for a year or two, with the option of reviewing it later and evaluating how successful it was. The theory behind your decisions is not nearly as important as how many future situations they wind up resolving to your satisfaction—just as the American Constitution is remarkable not so much for its political theorizing but for how flexible and comprehensive it has proven to be. So have all your wars right up front when you're writing the charter; later, your discussions can revolve around what decision is the proper one, not around who's in charge.

KEY ISSUES TO ADDRESS

s we've said, your charter can take any form, and be as long or short as you see fit. We'd encourage brevity—not only because it will make for a document people will actually use, but because forcing yourself to be concise will help you avoid over-complicated or vague procedures and responsibilities.

But don't let the goal of brevity deter you from writing a document that addresses the real issues of who is going to have the liturgical power in your parish. Even if, in your situation, it's painfully clear who already has this power, *write it down*. Force people to put their expectations and unspoken rules on paper. Your pastor or your music director may find it just a bit embarrassing to have a document around that gives him only slightly less authority than the Sun King.

So, however you choose to write it, make sure your charter covers the following points:

1. *Purpose of the committee.*
   Is your committee an advisory body to the pastor? Is its goal to articulate some solid guidelines by which the parish evaluates liturgy, or is it to provide some advice to the pastor on only those questions he chooses to delegate to it? What sorts of issues is it in business to decide, and which questions will be beyond its bailiwick? Are there any clear, specific goals for liturgy the parish is willing to articulate right now?

As we said earlier, it's unlikely that your charter will wind up giving your committee authority over the pastor, even though this is the way things may work out in practice, or though you may feel this is the way things should ultimately be. In the meantime, we think that in the process of creating this charter you should be leaning as much in the direction of autonomy as your circumstances permit.

Define as clear and as specific a role for your committee as possible. State exactly which topics the committee can decide on, either by vote or by consensus, and which topics the committee is entitled to prepare recommendations on. The very least your committee can do in areas in which it should have a lot to say (clergy skills and appropriateness of assignments, staff hiring and evaluation, general comments on the parish's liturgies and goals) is to stir things up, and the best way to do that is to write things down and circulate them. There should be no area of the parish's liturgical life on which your committee should not at least be entitled to submit annual recommendations and evaluations.

In the remainder of this book, as we discuss meetings and liturgy evaluation, we hope to give you some ideas that will make such reports more than just prejudiced opinionizing or bland approval of the status quo. In the meantime, just keep this in mind: The opinions of your committee will be far more difficult to ignore regularly—and you will have a very useful focus for your discussions—if regular reports are officially demanded by the charter of your committee.

2. Money.

Who will establish how much of the parish's money is spent on its liturgies? How binding will a recommendation of the liturgy committee be in this regard? Who will allocate this liturgy budget among the various possibilities? Who approves this decision? How public will all this information be, and how frequently will it be discussed?

It will be rare to find a parish where there aren't particular numbers which are, for some reason, considered confidential. Even a large parish that undertakes M.B.A.-level analysis of votive-light profitability can be reluctant to reveal the salary of its music director, even to its liturgy committee members.

At the very least, ask for disclosure. This is *your* money you're dealing with, and in the parish setting as in every other, money means power. If the liturgies in your parish are terrible, it will undoubtedly take money to improve them—money for music, for renovations, for visiting clergy, for new hymnals. You have to know how much these things cost, and how much your parish has to pay for them, to judge whether the parish is genuinely able to reallocate some resources in a new and desirable direction.

A simple example: If someone is arguing against a particular liturgical change, one argument may well emerge: Parishioners will be alienated, and a drop in collections is sure to follow. To discuss this intelligently (if that's possible) you may need to know what the collection at each of your liturgies is week by week; you should be able to defuse such money-based liturgical arguments, not by saying that money should have nothing to do with such things, but by having the facts at your fingertips. (You can also deflect them, as one committee member we know did, by tossing a $20 bill on the table whenever such a discussion came up, facetiously offering to pay for the change in question. This was always good for laughs, but probably not the best way to deal with the issue.)

Do remember one thing when dealing with money issues: You cannot divorce decision-making power from the power of the purse. There are vital liturgical communities that can't get $35 a week to pay a musician, and the liturgy flounders; the liturgy committee, it turns out, has nothing to say about who gets paid and who doesn't. There are parishes that pay a music director $10,000 a year to take care of one extravagant weekly liturgy; who decides that a much needed $5,000 chapel renovation is too expensive?

Unfortunately, even if you succeed in obtaining a detailed breakdown of your parish's expenditures on liturgy, and can see how extensive those expenditures are in relationship to other areas of expense and the parish's annual income, there is no clear rule of thumb that would enable you to argue for a particular level that might be defined as the norm. Suffice it to say that some parishes somehow find it possible to devote almost half their financial resources to professional soloists, singers, and musicians (none of whom may be making significant improvements in the quality of the parish's liturgies) while other parishes will bridle at the suggestion of allowing communion under both species, lest the altar-wine bill double or triple in one fell swoop.

Your committee's turf should include, at the very least, a review of the parish liturgy budget on an annual basis, with the opportunity to make recommendations on both the total amount and the budget's allocation. If you're lucky, your committee will have a few people with the financial savvy to formulate that budget and look at it every year from the ground up. Find the middle ground between, on the one hand, reducing every new liturgical idea to its economic impact and, on the other, pretending it's OK that your committee has no say about how money is spent. If your group has no real power in the budgeting process, it will quickly find that its chains to the liturgical status quo are heavy indeed.

3. Clergy.

Can the liturgy committee impose a requirement on parish clergy that they attend planning meetings for liturgies in which they will take part? Will a regular evaluation of clergy be a part of the committee's discussions? Will this information be public? Will a recommendation be binding? Or will all these issues by handled informally? Can the liturgy committee invite outside clergy to preside or preach, and can money be made available for this purpose? How open will this process be, and how often can comments be made on it?

Here again, committees will never have an official, enforceable voice. If your parish staff happens to be incompetent, hostile, or poor preachers, your liturgies will suffer a painful series of weekly pummelings.

Nevertheless, we think your committee should be putting its feelings on paper. The primary reason is simple: The work of your presiders is a (and, as we'll see later, perhaps *the*) prime determinant of how well your liturgy works. A strong presider and a moving homily have saved many a bad-news liturgy; enthusiastic music and careful planning have rarely made up for a sleepy presider, or one who offended through ignorance or inappropriateness.

We think you should have the right to comment officially and regularly on those who preside at your liturgies. Don't rely too much on subtle hints to get your message across. Build a system where the planning groups for each particular liturgy submit some notes on the presiders they've had, and where the parish committee—in spite of all the conflicts of opinion it is sure to bring up—writes an annual report on the subject. A regular evaluation will, in the long run, actually be *less* threatening, since the report is a matter of regular business and is less likely to be mistaken for a vendetta.

Hand in hand with this process will be comments on how clergy are assigned to a particular liturgy. Every pastor will have a different theory (or no theory at all) about the effectiveness of having the same presider at one liturgy week after week, or of seemingly random rotation based on clerical convenience. We won't advocate either position, since success depends far more on the personalities involved than on the specific system. Nevertheless, whatever system there is will be of critical importance; removing a regular presider from a liturgy can have a deadly effect on a growing community, and the assignment of a poor homilist to a congregation used to far better will have an immediate impact. Make sure that good long-term relationships have some way to continue, and that you have some leverage in the whole process. Make sure your comments are called for at various intervals.

This is a sensitive area, and you may feel that your reports and evaluations are unheard. But don't underestimate the long-term effects of steady and subtle pressure for change. The next time your parish is going to be assigned a new associate pastor, your pastor may find himself, to his surprise, asking the chancery office to make sure to send him someone who can preach.

4. *Personnel.*

How many positions can the parish create for the employment of professional liturgists or musicians? How much will they be paid? How will the search process be conducted, and whose decision is binding? How regularly will these people receive a formal evaluation, and from whom? Who will write a job description for these positions, one which details both the responsibilities of the job and to whom the position reports?

First, the question of job descriptions. We don't think a parish has any business hiring someone without a clear description of responsibilities, accountability and reporting relationships. Oh, but but we're only a little parish, you may say. What could possibly be a major issue?

Plenty. As soon as you or your parish hires anyone, you have, in effect, taken responsibility for someone's professional life for however long that person is employed by you. What's more, church musicians and liturgy directors are working in an area where job performance is enormously difficult to evaluate, and where the positions themselves are so new that clear reporting relationships have not had a chance to become "standard." As a consequence, liturgy professionals quickly find that they are either (a) accountable to no one for their style of leadership, their skill at performance, or their ability to work with anyone; or (b) scapegoats, immediately blamed for anything about a liturgy which someone doesn't like, evaluated far more on their ability to kow-tow than on liturgical talent, and whipsawed by conflicting judgments and evaluations.

Please give your employees a break. Have someone write up a description of what the person is supposed to do, and whose evaluation is binding. Preferably, this document will grow out of the needs of a particular liturgy or group of liturgies; members of these planning groups should describe in some detail what they expect in terms of musical flexibility, working style, professionalism, and personality. But even if it's only a piece of paper that a pastor writes up solo, we hope he remembers to define how much the liturgy committee—or a planning committee for a liturgy at which the staff person may be working—will have to say about that person's performance.

We think they should have plenty to say, restricted by only one rule: Evaluate that person based on *long-term* results compared to the *goals* you established at the outset. Don't allow the feeling that you have power over staff people to become a license to ride herd on them. If you don't like the job they're doing, the chances are about even that it's because you didn't really articulate what you wanted them to do in the first place.

One final thought. Catholics have come a long way in the past twenty years on the topic of unpaid musicians. The lesson of all this progress is clear: You get what you pay for. Not just in terms of talent and skills, but in terms of control and loyalty. People whom you pay are more likely to be talented; but it's also true that paying people obliges them to be reliable and committed, and obliges you to be respectful of their skills. Don't let your parish rely on finding good people who'll work for nothing, or allow your liturgies to be run by the wrong people just because they happen to come for free. Have your charter articulate a commitment to professionalism, and commit yourselves to searching out the right people. They're out there somewhere—run ads, ask around, and take your time.

> 5. *Relationship with subcommittees.*
> How will disputes between your parish committee and the committees you establish for each liturgy be resolved? What power does a parish liturgy committee have over the preferences of a particular community? How often will a parish evaluate its constituent liturgies, and what power do its reports have?

Here we enter a tricky area, and one where the particular history and personalities of your parish will play a large part. You may not have any liturgies where a well-established group has played a role in starting or perpetuating a particular style or custom of celebrating. In

There is nothing more offensive—or, unfortunately, common—than the anonymous note to the pastor, the bishop, or the apostolic delegate. You will be faced with such a confrontation someday, and your pastor may even be inclined to view it with some seriousness. *Please* build into your system some way of screening out those complaints that don't even have a name signed to them; you will be doing your part to raise the level of church life. Your pastor may feel that passing on anonymous comments to you is "discreet"— it isn't. It's a way of manipulating you into his own point of view, or helping him avoid a conflict he shouldn't be avoiding.

Do, however, make sure that legitimate, signed complaints concerning liturgies are both discussed by the parish committee regularly and *answered* by either the pastor or a committee member to whom this has been delegated.

that case, your job as a committee is, in a way, to start backwards, and try to build groups such as this at each of the liturgies your parish schedules.

But let's assume that you have at least one of these groups. It is inevitable that some sort of conflict will arise between an active liturgical planning group and the parish as a whole. Perhaps there will be a request for money, for additional staff, for a departure from standard parish procedure with respect to the offertory collection or altar boys; perhaps members of your parish committee will hear complaints about something that is going on at one of these liturgies, or even originate such complaints.

These issues should not be allowed to percolate beneath the surface, or be handled by means of closed-door reprimands. Your charter needs a system by which requests from a planning group are discussed and evaluated—at a meeting representative of the parish committee as a whole—and by which official complaints to the parish concerning rubrics or liturgical offenses are made public and discussed with the appropriate people present. (See "Your Secret Admirers," left).

How well liturgy planning groups are treated is related to some extent to how good a mix of folks you have on the parish committee, and we'll get to that in the next chapter. But it's also related to whether your parish committee actually has the power to make any decisions concerning money or personnel requests. There's a lot more grumbling about a request to the parish committee that is constantly deflected and ignored than one that gets a quick and honest "no"—with a straightforward explanation.

But will your parish ever be faced with a decision to shut down, change, thwart, or deny requests by a legitimate and easily identifiable community? That's very possible; perhaps your goals as a parish will require your committee to close down the Tridentine mass, or to renovate a folk group where there isn't a competent musician in the lot. We hope, however, that you will articulate in your charter that such a decision will be preceded only by the most agonizing reappraisal; that every representative involved will make a commitment to an extended period of talk, retreat, and examination of alternatives; that your liturgy chairperson has suggested every alternative short of a pilgrimage to Loretto. We don't want you to be afraid of a tough decision; but neither do we want you to toss out one single possibility for relocating, rescheduling, rearranging, improvement or compromise. Your primary job is encouraging a variety of liturgies to happen, not imposing uniformity where there doesn't need to be any.

6. *The liturgical schedule.*

What authority will the parish have with respect to how many liturgies the parish has, and when they take place? How often will such a decision be subject to revision?

As we've already said, we think talking about the schedule *as schedule* is one of the most boring possibilities for any committee, and that it's usually a red herring for a deeper conflict or a lack of ideas. If there is a serious and recurring problem with scheduling logistics, ask yourself: Does your parish have too many liturgies?

Nevertheless, we hope your parish committee's charter calls for an annual comment on the schedule—not so much from the point of view of parking convenience or sacristy traffic, but from that of variety and fullness. Are all our liturgies alike? Is there a demand for another type of liturgy? Are we exploring morning and evening prayer in addition to the eucharist? Could we use a midnight mass on Saturdays to attract a particular group? Are there liturgies at neighborhood parishes we could learn a thing or two from? *Here* are the real issues your committee should spend its time talking about; make sure your charter articulates this as a key piece of business. Better liturgies will, of course, require more resources, both clerical and financial; be realistic, but also make sure you're not running away from change.

The list doesn't end with these six items; the final two topics for your charter—membership and leadership—are deserving of their own chapters, and you'll get more than you need to know about them as you read on.

But before you proceed, allow us to reiterate how important this chapter you just finished actually is. Liturgy committees have a strong tendency to focus conflicts on people, personalities, and what purport to be questions of liturgical judgment. What is often *actually* going on is something else: a fight for turf. Think about the politics of your group before anything else. The groundwork for a successful committee begins right here.

Membership

At first, it may seem like a good idea to open up membership on your liturgy committee to anyone who happens to come forward, or who seems like a nice person, or who's new in the parish, or who did yeoman service in another parish organization. In this chapter, we hope to convince you otherwise, and to give you some ideas about how to get the people you *really* need.

Working on liturgy is different from the parish carnival, the community chest, or the altar society (whatever that is). Many parish activities, to be frank, require only physical labor, lots of time, and an enormous amount of good will. Liturgy evaluation and discussion, on the other hand, ideally require less time but a great deal of independent thinking.

Be honest. You have to admit that many parishioners are not the types to play a role that may require them to evaluate the parish's long-standing customs and staff members. The very idea is foreign to them. They may even be associated with the parish's volunteer activities simply because of their strong sense of territoriality—*my* parish. (Or, they may not have anything better to do.)

This is not to suggest that you are establishing a new hierarchy which systematically excludes certain groups. But we *are* saying that the ability to give honest, constructive criticism is not a gift shared by all—nor is musical talent, leadership, or the ability to give good homilies. Your liturgy committee needs these particular talents, not just hard or willing workers.

Remember one thing before you start your recruiting process. You've got two very different kinds of groups you need members for—the parish committee, and the planning groups. As we'll see, there will probably wind up being some overlap between these two, primarily because people who become active at one particular liturgy may eventually start working at the parish level as well. But one thing you'll probably notice immediately is that there are big differences in the types of people that get involved with these two sorts of groups, the *ways* they wind up joining, and how big the groups tend (or need) to get. Let's take the two groups separately.

THE PARISH COMMITTEE

The easiest way to think of the people who will make up the membership of your parish committee may be to picture two groups, both of which need to be fully represented:

1. *Those regularly involved in planning one of your parish's liturgies.* Everyone who is actively involved with working on a particular liturgy is entitled to a place on your parish committee, and each one of your planning groups needs to be represented. This probably means that all the people you pay to be your liturgists—musicians and other professionals—will be automatically invited to become members, and perhaps even required to be members as a condition of their employment.

Why is this a good thing? In the first place, because it will give you a core group of already active people—people who, even if they cannot yet articulate it, have an allegiance to a particular liturgy or liturgical style. Your primary challenge here will not be to get them to develop some clear likes and dislikes, but to get them to articulate the ones they already have.

Second, it will give you (we hope) at least two groups of people whose liturgical preferences are somewhat at odds. Perhaps you will find this conflict unproductive—it can easily become so. But we think it's preferable to having people who are there because it doesn't matter to them which liturgy they attend; after all, they like the mass. This will get very boring after a while.

Third, it's only fair. Your parish committee will, through its financial and personnel decisions, determine the future of the liturgies of your parish. The key people who have been working on these liturgies need to be heard regularly, and to hear what's being said about their work. If, for whatever reason, you find that the planning people at a particular liturgy have some aversion to participating in the parish group—either through some sort of anti-establishment prejudice or because of some particular historical incident—keep working on them, and keep reiterating the purposes and territory of your committee.

2. *Those parishioners whose temperament inclines them to the evaluation of liturgies.* Mixed in with your active liturgists, include a good number of people who may not devote time

each week to actual planning of a particular liturgy. But these are not to be thought of by any stretch of the imagination as "ordinary folks."

Review the job description we set out in Chapter One for a good liturgy committee member. Think about it carefully as you talk to people who have expressed an interest in membership, or as you read over the questionnaires you've devised to separate the pious from the perceptive. You want people who have opinions but not prejudices; people who may like one style of liturgy but are willing to sit still through a few others. You want people who are interested in seeing some particular things happen but are willing to let other people have their way, too—as long as that way isn't a genuine threat to the committee's goals for the parish's liturgies.

But articulate members like this are hard to find, and they're rare for two reasons. The first is that there just aren't that many people who've had a strong enough experience of good liturgy that would make them want to recreate that experience in another setting. Bad liturgy breeds indifferent Catholics; a strong liturgical community, on the other hand, will have enthusiastic alumni everywhere. Bad liturgy, however, is far more common than good.

The other reason such people are scarce is that, like most perceptive and articulate people, they're busy. Not busy with other parish activities, maybe, but just busy with their own lives, with a variety of other projects and interests they find rewarding. They are people who are inclined to articulate their likes and dislikes, and that means they're not inclined to sit still for something that wastes their time, no matter how admirable the purported goal. These are people it's tough to rope in for a weeknight meeting, but these are exactly the people you want.

How will you find them? By taking the opposite course of most parishes that need people to help out, which is latching on to those people who are still sitting around after everyone else leaves. You need to make your group seem a desirable one—one which has a clear goal, and clear responsibilities; one where people's time is not abused; one which clearly has an effect on liturgies; one which fosters friendships and fun.

You'll communicate these things primarily by doing them; a successful group accomplishing things and enjoying themselves will quickly attract others by word of mouth. But suppose you're just now trying to get some fresh blood into your committee. Keep two points in mind as an ongoing public-relations program for your group:

1. Write your announcements and membership pitches with a great deal of care. Don't be vague, don't be condescending, and don't be (overtly) theological. Give examples of what the committee has accomplished. Say how long the meetings are, and how often they are. Imply that the material for discussion is substantive, and not limited to issues of scheduling, decorations, logistics, lectoring, or who'll help out on Holy Thursday. Say who's on the committee, and how big the group is. Hand out your job description. Don't settle for a bald announcement of the liturgy committee's next meeting date and time—if you're going to bother to announce it at all, give people a reason to come. Don't take yourselves too seriously (people get enough of that at their regular jobs). (See sample pitches at right.) And keep your announcements and invitations coming regularly; some of your most valuable potential members may be busy enough (or liturgically perceptive enough) to be only occasional visitors to your parish, and may miss your perfunctory annual announcement.

2. Offer some interesting limited commitments on a regular basis. If your liturgy committee has a reading list (see Appendix), offer the books for sale parish-wide. If you're going to go on an unusual field trip, invite people to come along as guests. Have your committee members (wearing name tags) occasionally visit each parish liturgy and hang around afterwards to meet people. Keep thinking of ways to make your parish committee sound busy, challenging, and full of potential friends.

Sample Pitches

BAD PITCH

The Liturgy Committee meeting will be held two weeks from this Tuesday night at 7:30 in the rectory. All are welcome.

LONGER BUT BETTER PITCH

The Parish Liturgy Committee will have its regular monthly meeting this Tuesday night in the rectory. We'll discuss the possibility of establishing daily morning prayer, and form a small group to plan and evaluate our parish's Holy Week celebrations. Meetings are informal (there are only twelve of us) and last no more than an hour. Those who come just to listen may well decide to ask how to become a member—after all, the food isn't half bad. The committee's chairperson is Bub Muldoon [Bub's phone number goes here].

STARTING UP A NEW GROUP

The toughest question is how to get a new committee going from scratch. Suppose you're a pastor, an associate, a music director or a parish council member—and you're faced with the need to start from zero (or one: you). Where do you begin?

As with many organizational issues in this book, we can't really lay down any hard and fast rules. You know your parish, your staff, and your history better than we do. Nevertheless, here are a few guidelines and truisms you may find useful as you set off down that lonesome road.

How big?

The size of your group should reflect its function—in general, small groups *do*, and big groups *think*. This principle applies to both your parish committee and your planning groups.

We think *planning* a liturgy is what the psychologists call a disjunctive task[1]—a job where the results depends more on creative talent and skills than on brute force. In disjunctive tasks, the end result is only as good as the most talented individual member of the group—which means that adding in a lot of people making little contribution will not make the group, or its work, any better. Don't let your recruiting efforts for planning groups let you wind up with a lot of people whose presence only slows things down.

In the parish committee, though, since the tasks involve more representation and evaluation than creative work, theoretically you could use a bigger group—a big enough group to get a wide variety of viewpoints. (In a planning group, on the other hand, *less* variety may help an individual liturgy develop its own style and strengths.) Six to ten is a good size to shoot for at first—because the bigger your parish committee gets, the more problems you'll face. For one thing, people *prefer* to work in smaller groups; while big groups mean a greater chance that someone will find someone in the group they like and thus be inclined to stick around, they also mean that people are far less inclined to make a significant contribution.[2] In addition, the bigger the group, and the more diverse it becomes, the stronger the leadership you need to get things done.

Yet while we hope you decide to start small, we hope you don't let our warnings about group size blind you to an even greater danger—the fear of new people. Some groups—like yours, if you're starting from nothing—are desperate for new members. Others, for a variety of reasons, regard them as a threat, because they interrupt business as usual. In a polarized group, new people can change the chemistry and cause old coalitions to be re-formed; in a

1. This even applies to churches. One study of five sociologically similar Milwaukee Methodist parishes found that members of the smaller communities participated in more different kinds of activities, held more leadership positions, spent more time in parish activities, attended church more often, and even contributed more money. Allan W. Wicker, "Size of Church Membership and Members' Support of Church Behavior Settings," *Journal of Personality and Social Psychology* 13 (1969) 278-288.

2. Marvin E. Shaw, *Group Dynamics*, second edition (New York: McGraw-Hill, 1976), pp. 320-321.

homogeneous group they may just not seem to fit in to what has become a very comfortable parish social club. Any group that doesn't want a fairly steady flow of old people leaving and new people coming in is showing signs of degeneration—be on guard for it.

Who's on first?

No matter how desperate your situation, you'll probably be able to start out with several people who have a vested interest in your liturgical situation: a musician or two, and perhaps an active (and excellent) lector. That gives you four members, unless you're one of the above. Between the four of you, surely you can find two others—but don't act hastily, or out of desperation. Look for people you think would be effective, not people who'll fill seats. At this stage, finding a solid core group of congenial people is crucial; don't feel bad if you haven't been open about the selection process, as long as it means that you're starting strong.

If you need to put out an ad—don't automatically accept anyone who answers it. Invite people who express an interest to a meeting or two as observers—perhaps you'll even ask them to fill out a questionnaire based on your job description, or at least take them out for a drink and talk it over. After that, the committee can decide whether it would like to extend an invitation to join.

And in general, in spite of whatever pressure you may feel to add particular people to your committee, or simply to get new faces, this is a pattern you will find useful throughout all the stages of your group's development: (1) new member attends a few meetings; (2) formal or informal review process; (3) invitation to join. Breaking down all the barriers to membership may seem like a good or a fair idea—but in fact it only threatens to water down your group with nonparticipating members, and prevents a committee from developing a sense of its own special qualifications and expertise for the job at hand. If you'll take anybody who shows up—what does that say about the people who are already there?

What about the clergy?

Now, another natural for any committee: the clergy. Maybe the pastor and all the staff? And maybe . . . whoooa.

Our advice—perhaps controversial—is in most cases *not yet*.

Yes, you will of course want them in the long run—and if one of your parish clergy is the driving force behind your committee, it may be a fait accompli. But take a closer look at what might, and in all too many cases *does*, happen.

You have a new committee that's just going to be learning about liturgy, feeling its way, trying to develop a sense of its own range of opinions. Then you introduce a priest who everyone sort of assumes has had some sort of liturgical training somewhere along the line. That can be a good thing—depending on the priest. But it can also be very dangerous to your group's organizational childhood. Couple the priest's assumed *expertise* and the *leadership* role many will automatically grant him, and you just got Father Lipski's liturgy committee, and not yours, or your parish's.

Try to get going on your own first. Get your original group together and have a few brainstorming sessions about what's right (or wrong) with your liturgies. Read some books together (like this one). Visit some "great" liturgies nearby and talk about them among yourselves. Then start to consider your parish's liturgies more seriously—and then, and only then, invite some members of your parish's staff along to participate. If they're helpful and non-directive, great; if you don't find their participation useful, there should be nothing in your system (or your charter) that says you have to vote in someone you don't want, or who isn't entitled to a spot because of specific liturgical responsibilities in the parish.

All this is much less critical for a group that's had a chance to get going—they may be accustomed to criticizing the activities of the clergy as well as making use of whatever expertise and insights they have. It's also not to say that priests can't function successfully as a committee's resident experts, or even as "ordinary" members—of course, they can (and do). But a new group, unsure of itself, is almost sure to take the easy way out and follow Father's advice. Father, if you're listening, restrain yourself.

All the caveats we've listed above also apply to any sort of "experts" in your parish—from the organist with a master's degree from Juilliard to the sister who once went to a weekend liturgy workshop. The key issue here, as with the clergy, is separating the concept of leadership from that of expertise. Your leaders (as we'll discuss in the next chapter) need to know what expertise *is*, but don't have to *be* experts; your experts, by the same token, are not necessarily the people who need to be your leaders (and often *shouldn't* be).

Liturgy committees need experts: to tell them about

music, to know the rules, to preach, write, and sing. But the goal in liturgy committee membership is not to defer to the experts but to use them, learn from them, and perhaps even become one yourself. When an expert is also the person in power, this process is thwarted. First, because someone who seems like they know what they're talking about is automatically given power by members of the group. And when that person is, *in addition*, nominally in charge, there will be a natural tendency for others to neglect even further their responsibility to learn and contribute. The result: A few experts doing all the talking, and a lot of other people listening—if they bother to stick around at all.

This danger of setting up a little society of experts and drones is a very real one. The only solution is to give the whole issue of membership development constant attention. How? Start by creating opportunities for "regular" members to work one-on-one with the experts—form small discussion or research teams to examine particular questions. Don't always defer questions to the experts ("Monsignor, is there a rule against that?")—ask someone else to master the documents and regulations. If you work at it imaginatively, you'll wind up with a committee where everyone's learning, not a poorly attended monthly lecture on liturgy.

Cleaning house

A situation akin to starting from scratch is when you wish you *could* start from scratch. Suppose you're a new pastor or chairperson, and you're faced with a contentious group with a long history of conflict that has caused a permanent stall. Or a group where the entrenched majority never stops playing their favorite tunes. Or a group that *looks* bored but is actually quite happy in its inactivity. What to do?

Naturally, some creative conflict (see Chapter Four) is the first thing to try. A brace of new members, some unusual agendas, and a little confrontation may work wonders. But if you genuinely feel that the situation is not salvageable, we think you should face facts, and start from square one. Put everyone on notice, set up some membership criteria, and build the kind of group you need.

Naturally, this is buying you a lot of trouble—existing members will run to the pastor, exert pressure, write letters, and put up quite a fight. Our only advice is to *stick with the process once you have begun it*. It's far worse to have to try to smooth over an event like this if it's somehow stopped in the middle—if you're forced to back down, your leadership has suffered a terminal blow to its credibility. Reach an understanding with your pastor *beforehand* about how much trouble there's likely to be, and make sure that he (or your parish council) won't pull the rug out from under you once the fighting starts.

THE PLANNING GROUPS

In forming a planning group for a particular liturgy, part of the search process is done for you. The hardest part isn't.

The easy half

For starters, any liturgy you are taking seriously enough to consider establishing a planning group for will have, we hope, at least one staff member (perhaps a musician) who has that liturgy as a responsibility. If the person is one of your paid musicians, attendance at the planning group's meeting should be a clearly stated condition of that person's employment. Importing musicians to lead music selected by others, or selecting music without reference to the other liturgical planning going on, is a bad practice. You don't need to take our word for it: Ask anyone who begins to take weekly liturgical planning seriously, and then has to deal with a musician not part of the long-term process of talking about what that liturgy is supposed to be like. Don't say we didn't warn you.

As a second planning group member, you may also have the presider at the liturgy—perhaps one priest who will be celebrating with you regularly. Contrary to everything we said in the previous section concerning the clergy, having a presider at every planning meeting is crucial for the long-term success of that liturgy. Not because homilies have to reflect what was said at the planning meeting, or because that's the only place where fine points of coordination, detail, and logistics can be worked out. It's because the presider, more than any other single individual, has the power to make or break that liturgy. The chances of not breaking it are immeasurably improved if the presider knows what that liturgy is trying to do, contributes to its creation, and has the benefit of regular, honest feedback.

Every liturgy, then, will probably start out with two people who are getting paid to plan it. If disaster strikes—if no one else shows up—at least you have people who will make sure things happen.

But, as we said in the last section, that's just not going to be enough. Not just because these two can't go it alone— we suppose it's possible to have a presider and music director so talented, with so much energy, and so perceptive of a community's needs, that they could between the two of them come up with a genuinely outstanding liturgy week after week. But that's unlikely—and even if it weren't, there are a few other people from the community they need to talk with before they go off and do their respective things.

The tough half

The people they need to talk with aren't there simply to guard against a steady diet of objectionable imports (Josquin motets, Carey Landry, whatever). While these community members may act as a check on creativity run wild, that is not their primary function. Neither should they be included simply to instill a sense of lay leadership or ownership, although that is a fine side effect to shoot for. The real reason is that liturgy is the prayer of the community—prayer that has elements of show biz, and prayer that often requires expert guidance, but first and foremost the community's prayer of celebration. That means some people from that community need to work on it. It is their property. It is their responsibility. Anything that gets planned without them is only a show.

We hope you found that last bit inspiring—because now we have the bad news: Many liturgies die, flounder, and remain stagnant because they lack good planning group members like these.

The reason is simple: You have a finite group of people as your pool of potential members, and that's the people who are already attending that liturgy. The trouble is, look at your congregation: By and large, their reasons for being there don't immediately suggest that they would be interested in *planning* that liturgy. You have people who are devoted attenders of your liturgy but have absolutely no interest in how it all happens. You have people who come each week—but who, it turns out, hate that liturgy but would come to anything that fit their schedule. You'll have a lot of people—probably the majority—who are not quite sure why they're there in the first place, and would therefore be extremely uncomfortable with the idea of discussing liturgy with strangers who, presumably, are on top of things religiously.

In that group, it's unlikely that you will find someone who has had a good liturgical experience somewhere else, who has had any experience reading and discussing scripture with other people, or who has any idea what sort of things can be done with the raw material of the liturgy. If there's someone like that out there, we hope you are lucky enough to grab them. If, week after week, you just don't see anyone like that, you have only one choice, and that's to set out on the road to developing such people yourself.

A long search

As we mentioned in our earlier discussion about group size, you don't need an awful lot of people to have a successful planning group—as few as two people in addition to your presider and musical leader can make an outstanding team. But inciting people to make the transition from congregation member (traditionally passive) to planner (active, we hope, and working hard at a weekly meeting) is a genuine challenge—far more difficult than forming a parish committee out of already active planning groups. Let's have a look at the two major obstacles that stand in the way of your effort, and how to overcome them.

1. People have no idea that liturgies are planned. Hey look, can you blame people for thinking this? Given that most liturgies people have seen have probably looked like a series of clerical still lifes, with the primary visual image one of priests reading from big books, it isn't surprising that folks can't imagine that any real thought went into it behind the scenes. Isn't it all done by rote? Do you mean there are *choices*?

We might be exaggerating, but we don't think so. Most people just don't realize the *variety* of ways a liturgy can feel, and all the things that work together to create those feelings, because *they've never seen it at work*. As we said earlier, good liturgy spawns people who want more good liturgy, and are willing to work for it; if you are a pastor, presider, or musician trying to form a planning group, please realize that your most important job may be simply communicating that work *does* go into what you do.

You'll do this primarily through the liturgy itself: You may not think that good liturgy is noticed, but it is. People are not stupid; neither are they insensitive when other people actually seem to be paying attention to them while they are sitting in the pews. When they begin to realize that there are such things as liturgical seasons; when they are handed congregational aids and bulletins that look as though a little thought went into them; when people talk to them, greet them, shake their hand and remember their names—the people who care, and who will be your future planning group members, will notice.

You can help those people who actually grow to like your liturgy by telling them, both on a one-to-one basis and through announcements, that there is a planning group for that liturgy that meets regularly. While we think personal contact will, in the setting of one particular congregation, be more effective in obtaining the big commitment of time and energy you'll need, there's a lot to be said for clear, detailed, and regular announcements of what a liturgical planning meeting is like. Follow some of the same suggestions we made for recruiting for your parish committee—remember that people who consider themselves basically untrained in scripture and liturgy will need concrete examples of what they can contribute.

With announcements, you may generate a long procession of people who come to a meeting out of good will and don't return. Planning meetings are often scripture-centered, and many can be intimidated (or bored) by such small-group discussions. The only solution is to keep trying—and take a quick look to see if your meetings really *aren't* getting a little intimidating or boring.

2. People don't know who's involved in planning the liturgy.
Just as people can't imagine *what* goes on in planning, they probably have a hard time picturing that there's a group—a community—involved with doing it.

When your liturgies go from week to week with no people in evidence except the presider and maybe a nervous lector, you have to realize that this probably doesn't look like a vital process in the works. The issue here is not just participation but *visibility*—people in your congregation need to perceive that a regular group of people is involved, on a regular basis, in working on this liturgy.

Most of the things involved in communicating this aren't recruiting tricks—they are simply symptoms (and causes) of good liturgy. For instance, even if you only have a presider, a regular lector, and a music director involved—does everyone know their names? How about the people who are eucharistic ministers—can they be seated with the assembly, rather than on display way up front? Can they be there regularly enough to become familiar faces? (The custom of rotating lectors and eucharistic ministers through a variety of parish liturgies can become a needless barrier to community building.) Can you make sure that people are greeted before liturgies, and offered coffee afterwards, by the *same* group of individuals? Are you making sure that the names of people already involved with your liturgy are occasionally evident? Can you think of ways that people can meet others face to face, in some context other than a quick handshake on the church steps?

You can try all these things and others besides—and you may *still* not come up with a group that somehow catches fire. But keep at it: Having a small group like this at each liturgy will form the foundation of your parish's liturgical life. It will also be the most difficult thing this book asks you to do. Once you've decided to try, don't be discouraged. You are doing noble work—and at least you can take comfort in the assurance that, believe us, it isn't easy anywhere.

Leadership

nfortunately, the political and membership processes we've dealt with in the previous two chapters still require you to find outstanding people to lead your committees—particularly your parish committee. As we've suggested, your planning groups will be smaller, and thus better able to rely on a sense of collegiality and common purpose; a formal leadership role for a particular member may not be necessary in all cases. But for your larger and (we hope) more diverse parish committee, the role of your leaders is demanding enough to merit a chapter unto itself.

Notice that we seem to be using the word "leader" interchangeably with that of "chairperson"—that's intentional. We think your chairpeople should do just that, *lead*—that means being constantly active in motivating (and even manipulating) your members, and in shaping the outcome and direction of your committee's work.

This may violate your own mental picture of what a committee chairperson should be. Perhaps you've been influenced by parliamentary procedure, where a chairperson has a clearly defined role; in that context, chairing meetings often seems limited to recognizing the next speaker, or knowing what the rulebook says is supposed to happen next. Or, perhaps your role model for a good chairperson is someone who's a good note-taker, or a meeting convener, or a Great Compromiser.

In the setting of a liturgy committee, these models just aren't going to be good enough. As you've probably noticed already, discussing liturgy is a touchy business; without pushing, serious discussion just won't happen. The recurring problems of liturgy committees—constant conflict and unendurable focus on trivia—exist because *the group is not being managed well*.

It's tough enough to get people to work together in a business setting. In liturgy, where people on the one hand react powerfully to change and on the other are reticent about discussing and participating, you've got even more work cut out for you. A passive, yea-or-nay meeting format will only serve to keep emotional conflicts simmering below the surface while people focus on the votable. Weak, timid leadership means that the group wanders aimlessly through discussions that somehow never have a single visible effect on a parish's liturgies. We hope to make it clear in this chapter that leadership of a liturgy group is *not* a passive role—setting the time for the next meeting, taking minutes, or buying the Maxwell House.

Go back to the beginning of Chapter One and take a look at the terrible (but typical) meeting situations we described. Every one of them could have been avoided or nipped in the bud with a quick directive from the chair: This isn't our business. Let's defer this. We need to go on to other things. We resolved this last week. Let's leave it alone for a while. Let's save this for our annual review.

Sound a little overbearing? It can be—but from the right person, it won't be.

The danger isn't too much leadership but too much needless muscle-flexing. Consider the case of the chairperson who decides that a parish job is the ideal setting for doing what real-life big shots do: making decisions, choosing among options presented by various subordinates, criticizing. In this scenario, parishioners who have been real-life middle managers a bit too long get to work out their daytime frustrations. The trouble is, this *isn't* what real managers do—at least, it's not what the effective ones do.

In business, as well as the liturgy committee, the real responsibility of the person in charge is to make it possible for everyone else to be as productive as they can be. Chairpeople are at liturgy meetings to motivate people, to cut through the garbage and trivia, to get discussions back on track and done with, to help people make a good contribution and feel satisfied. And in fact, that's a much harder job than just making decisions.

It should be obvious, though, that what we are proposing for liturgy committee governance is not very much like democracy. In fact, we think voting per se should play a very small part in a committee's deliberations. The job of a chairperson is not to supervise a democratic process—it's to make sure the committee gets its job done. Part of that job *is* to make sure that everybody is heard, and that major decisions reflect to some extent the consensus of the group. But how well that gets done has very little to do with a careful "hands-off" attitude and a great deal to do with how well a chairperson has done groundwork before the meeting even starts, and how well he or she has established the goals for a particular meeting at the outset.

In fact, *the power to set the agenda* is probably the chairperson's single most important tool in running a successful group, and we'll address this issue more fully in the next chapter. First, there's the question of the *process* you use to choose the person you need to do the job.

FINDING THE RIGHT PERSON

A group's first chairperson will inevitably be chosen by the pastor, or by the first few stalwart members of the committee. How you evaluate, elect, draft, re-elect, or coronate this person's successors is really up to the group that writes your committee's charter. As they do so, there are two key issues they need to weigh—issues for which we have no easy answers.

First, there's the question of how long a chairperson should serve. There are advantages to limited terms of office and regular rotation—the main one is that it's easier to get rid of a dud or a puppet. Groups shouldn't be shackled to someone who turns out not to be a good leader, or who just isn't doing the job, and required retirement means that a group can, at the very least, wait around for parole. But the benefits of this safety net may well be outweighed by those of having a *good* person in for an extended run—long tenure can bring a thorough knowledge of the group's personality and give someone a chance to become truly outstanding at the job.

And *second*, there's the issue of democratic elections. Allowing a group to choose its own chairperson at regular intervals has the clear advantages of fairness and group acceptance. Adults are entitled to elect their own leaders, and they will feel better about a group in which this autonomy and judgment is recognized. In addition, in situations where the pastor or parish council imposes a choice, there is always the danger the the group will always be led by Father's Favorites—who may or may not be people the group will respect. But there are dangers with democracy, too—it can lead to too much turnover, with no one getting a chance to establish a genuine leadership role. It also assumes that people know what's good for them, and there are some committee situations in which Father *would* know best. A comatose group may well need a leader they'd never choose on their own, and a crafty pastor with a good candidate he wants in charge may need to subvert the democratic process to shake things up.

When your charter addresses these and other issues concerning where subsequent chairpeople are to come from, you will inevitably take your parish's own history, personalities, and past squabbles into account. But no matter which *system* you decide to try, there are certain *expectations* you need to write down. Being chairperson of your parish committee is a job, and you need to do the same thing you'd do for anybody in your parish with a job: Write a job description, with some clear areas of accountability and responsibilities.

What skills does the position of chairperson require?

What are the goals against which someone will be evaluated?

Who evaluates the person, and how often?

Who hires and fires, and on what grounds?

THE SKILLS YOU NEED

You probably can't write such a job description until you've given some thought to exactly *what* good chairpeople do. The first step may simply be to realize that there are, in fact, qualifications for the job.

Your chairperson should not *necessarily* be the person who has been with the group the longest, the person who is the best-educated, the person who has the best professional reputation, or the person who knows the most about liturgy. It's also not necessary for the chair to be occupied by the person who simply has more time available than anyone else—lots of extra time isn't always required. Such factors—education, longevity, popularity—will have *something* to do with how well your chairperson will do at being in charge, but they aren't the secret of success:

> **Your leader should be the person who will do the best job of keeping the group moving.**

Such a person will probably be outgoing, fair, and talkative, and very sensitive to the issue of using time well. But above all, this will be someone *impatient with old business*—and if your group just wants to keep things the way they are, you don't need a liturgy committee *or* a good chairperson.

The skills a liturgy chairperson needs to keep a group moving aren't easily taught, or often recognized for what they are: *Skills*. To remind chairpeople that what they have is a very complex assignment—and perhaps to help a parish staff or committee to size up potential leaders—we've devised a short analysis of the things liturgy chairpeople ought to be spending their time on, along with some friendly advice about how to handle the group they're responsible for.

1.● You need to be a good host.

In most respects, meetings are not like parties, but in one important respect they are: Successful meetings need just as much attention to the details of setting and hospitality as good parties. As chairperson, you are in charge of what one author on management calls "climate making"[1]—providing a setting in which everyone can feel at ease, work efficiently, think clearly, and have a good time.

Can you keep conversation moving when it starts to flag? Can you make people feel welcome when they walk in? Do you remember names, faces, and personal details? Do you pay careful attention to people's reactions? Do you know when people aren't having a good time? Can you get people who are not contributing interested in some particular topic or project?

All this is really only common courtesy—you'd care about these things if you were throwing a party in your own home. Nevertheless, it's surprising how many people seem to feel that the word "meeting" means that these little niceties can be dispensed with. If you do nothing else as chairperson, you can at least be polite—not just to be a nice guy, but because indifferent chairpeople set an immediately indifferent tone for the proceedings. Why should your members care, if you act like you don't?

In addition, as host you're in charge of setting a meeting place and time. This can have as much of an effect on your committee's motivational level as any other thing you do. It's appalling to think how many meetings take place in stuffy, dark church offices; thirty minutes without light or fresh air can hypnotize even the liveliest group. As evidence of even greater masochism, some committees decide to meet in unused school classrooms—where the chairperson (who, because of his or her position at the head of the room, is immediately awarded the subconscious role of teacher) faces the absurd sight of adults crammed into little desks and chairs. This is a meeting?

1. Franklyn S. Haiman, *Group Leadership and Democratic Action* (Boston: Houghton Mifflin, 1951).

You are asking people to do work, and people work better under good conditions. *Details count.* Find a bright, well-ventilated room. And make it a room with a big table—tables get the message across that you are there to accomplish things, and they also make it easier for people to refer to and pass around books and papers. If possible, get a round table; it sounds silly, but rectangular tables really do give the people who wind up seated at the ends an added element of power no matter what their official role.

Make your meeting room a friendly and comfortable place—coffee, dessert, and things to drink are great. But don't make it so comfortable and convivial (see "Home Sweet Home," right) that it takes a half hour beyond your scheduled time to get everyone to stop talking and call the meeting to order. Set the scene so that people are comfortable and can have some fun, but are also encouraged to get things done briskly. The real recreation time should be afterwards—it's a great incentive to get the meeting done with early.

2. You must be good at describing and verbalizing.

This is a very difficult skill to define—but it is the one which, perhaps more than any other, can keep a meeting on track.

Why? On the one hand, because a good describer and summarizer serves as a role model for the other members of the group, and sets a tone for all its discussions. The key business of your committee, after all, is articulating reactions and evaluations—someone who can, in turn, listen to someone's inarticulate or overly emotional reaction and *turn it into something that can be talked about* is a rare leader indeed.

Secondly, the skills of repeating and articulating help enormously in managing whatever conflicts on liturgical matters erupt. Chairpeople can help defuse many a heated argument by serving as the person who repeats, rephrases, and subtly reshapes what is going on. People in an argument are rarely arguing about what they *say* they're arguing about. By carefully repeating and expanding on what they are saying, you don't just wear them down—you help focus the issue in a way that may be helpful to the group. In addition, a chairperson who can stay calm and keep describing helps provide a sense that the conflict in question is not an all-enveloping or unmanageable one. Without that sense, a simple conflict can pick up speed as fast as a

Home Sweet Home

Some liturgy groups whose members become close friends schedule meetings over dinner or drinks at someone's house or apartment. While this sort of closeness is a fine thing to shoot for, chairpeople should insist on doing business in a neutral setting.

First, meeting rooms (if well equipped) are better than living rooms for imposing a certain discipline on discussions; they communicate to the group that you're there to concentrate and not to let the discussion wander. (*You* may feel like shooting the bull, but others in your group may not be in the mood to kill a whole evening every time you meet.) Second—and again, this may sound silly to you—people who host a meeting in their home, particularly if they do it regularly, acquire a certain extra degree of power in the group whether they realize it or not. They become de facto leaders—and why complicate the issue of who's in charge? Third, there's the simple question of making new members feel comfortable. While opinions may differ, many committee members will, when joining a group for the first time, find coming to someone's private home an additional barrier that compounds the already existing challenge of joining a new group. Home meetings may thus wind up excluding people who may not already be your friends.

Please don't get us wrong. We think every meeting, even in a meeting room, should have refreshments and comfortable chairs, and regular dinners together are a great idea. But we hope you decide to separate the actual meeting portion of the work from the socializing.

boulder rolling downhill.

The skill of describing and reflecting is not an easy one to develop. Examples might only mislead you, and are no substitute for watching someone who's good at it in action. Plenty of people *try* to be good articulaters; most of them wind up sounding like the stereotypical California therapist, parroting back every comment prefaced by "What I hear you saying is . . . " You're not supposed to be a shrink; you are supposed to help people say what they really mean, and defuse overheated conflict by clarifying the real issues at stake. When selecting a chairperson, don't look for someone who does the best job of saying what's agreeable to everyone, but someone who says things in a way that puts the issues in a new light.

Since the chairperson needs to play the role of chief repeater and verbalizer for the group, it's obvious that the pitfall is engaging in what's called defensive communication— evaluating, rather than describing, what you see going on in the meeting. Slipping from description into evaluation is easy, and the differences are subtle. Since you are bound to have opinions about most of the issues under discussion (and about the people you're listening to), you'll have a constant tendency to let those opinions slip.

No one's saying you can't keep those opinions. But if you're going to describe them, do just that—describe *your* feelings and opinions, don't evaluate someone else's. Perhaps you've noticed, either at work or at home, how many more good ideas seem to emerge when they aren't immediately met with critical evaluation. Good ideas are what your committee is in business to bring out. That means they're worth keeping your mouth shut for.

3. You are in charge of finding the expertise and resources your group needs.

It is not necessary for a liturgy chairperson to be the most liturgically knowledgeable member of the group (in fact, as we suggested in Chapter Three, it's probably best that he or she *not* be). But there is an important need for the chairperson to know the subject of liturgy well enough to distinguish expertise from hokum, and to know where to go to get answers and resources. Everyone on your committee should be taking time to educate themselves on liturgy— going to liturgies, reading, even traveling. It's important for the chairperson to do this too, but in his or her case the goal is identifying for future reference those resources the committee might find useful.

Examples: If your diocese has a liturgy office, your chairperson should meet the people there, know their strengths and weaknesses, and find out if there are any services or funds the parish might want to make use of. What about your neighboring parishes? It's invaluable for your chairperson to have a few contacts there—not just because they may be useful when you're involved in a personnel search, but for what might be called competitive information: What kind of music do they have? How much do they pay their musicians? What are *their* problems?

Chairpeople need to start their own little files and lists on a variety of topics. The Catholic church doesn't have a very good system of referring you to the people you'll need to advise you or do professional work for you; as chairperson, you'll have to do that yourself. When you see a successful church renovation, or an attractive set of altar vessels, find out who was responsible and *file it away*. When you hear a terrific music group somewhere else in town, go meet them and find out if they have friends who might be available to work in your parish. Are you on the mailing lists of all the people who publish liturgical music and books? Do you hear about all the workshops and courses in your area? Chairpeople have to like to collect information—and they need to recognize that parishes will never survive by being parochial.

Even within the committee itself, chairpeople need to develop the resources they need, and build them if they don't already have them. If an issue comes up in a meeting about what's liturgically "legal" and what isn't, you, as chairperson, are going to have to have somewhere to turn for an answer, and you're going to want to have confidence that you're not being sold a bill of goods. If that means knowing the liturgy documents yourself, then learn them. If it means finding someone you can trust who *does* know them, that's fine too. Just remember that finding and nurturing experts within the group is part of the job.

4.

You are in charge of managing the group's level of conflict.

Notice that we said *managing* conflict—not avoiding it.

> Any action that requires open struggle is in almost all cases undesirable, and results in clouding and misconstruing the idea and value of conflict.[2]

The first part of that statement is probably dear to the heart of most chairpeople—they think their job is to prevent, delay, and even paper over conflict on liturgical matters. And when it's *open* conflict—meaning bitter, personal, unproductive conflict, they're obviously right. Open conflict does nothing for your community, your liturgies, or your immortal souls.

But take a look at the second part of that statement, the controversial part. It implies that *conflict has value*. Groups without conflict are as tiresome and unproductive as faith without doubt. Most committees without a good scrap now and then about a substantive issue have probably reached this state of nirvana by carefully avoiding any discussion that might be regarded as interesting.

Part of the chairperson's job is to take constant readings on conflict—to start up a bit of a row where there isn't one, to get serious conflict out of the meeting (where it can only cause damage), and to identify the real conflicts where, on the surface, there is only petty squabbling about details and personalities. To help in this process, there are two secret weapons.

Creative troublemaking. Chairpeople should react against smugness, boredom, and inactivity at the earliest opportunity. Be sly. Place some new topics on the agenda—and include a few that some people will find threatening. Keep people off balance by asking them to participate in activities that they aren't usually a part of—or to attend a liturgy for which they do not particularly care. In the midst of one of the group's favorite arguments, propose a truly outrageous solution. Assign some reading you think many people will disagree with. Ask the unexpected question. All these things can be accomplished without

---

2. Stephen P. Robbins, *Managing Organizational Conflict* (Englewood Cliffs: Prentice-Hall, 1974), p. 23. An outstanding book if you're interested in the idea of creative conflict.

vitriol, without personal affront, and without ruining your credibility—if they're done sparingly, and only when you get the real sense that things need to be shaken up.

Conflict management. Meetings are not for arguing. They are not for hammering out compromises. They are for allocating resources, for establishing a sense of common purpose, and most importantly, for assigning work to the people who will actually get things done.

Your first defense against most unproductive conflict—as we've said repeatedly—is to set the boundaries for your committee's work before you even begin the meeting. Most fights are about things that are not the committee's business—or are not the committee's business at that particular meeting. If it's not on the agenda, if it's not an area defined in your committee's charter, if it's a matter that belongs to one of your planning groups, assert your authority and get the discussion over with.

The goal is to get serious conflict *out of big groups*; meetings where destructive conflict isn't snuffed out when it starts are like a dry forest waiting for a match. When you see an unresolvable argument erupting—about liturgical change, about personalities, about whatever your group loves to fight about—what you want to do nine times out of ten is get it off the floor and get it resolved privately.

Chairpeople, confronted by what has become an angry mob, can take a variety of actions, but most important are what might be called the pacification skills. Watch an experienced conflict manager in a tense situation; he or she will probably simply begin describing how they feel (tense, under pressure, upset). On the surface, this seems ridiculous—after all, who really cares? Yet there is method in the madness. In the first place it gets some statements out onto the floor that no one can disagree with—in the heat of an argument, this is no small accomplishment. In the second place, it slows things down; as statements that are by definition non sequiturs, descriptions of how *you* feel get some people thinking about how *they* feel—or maybe even feeling sorry for you, since you say you are feeling so bad. Third, it gives you a chance to propose that where the conflict really needs to be resolved is after the meeting—by a small group of those involved, by you and an individual privately, or by a third party. At the next meeting of the group, you can discuss how the issue has been resolved, or propose some concrete choices to the group.

This fast footwork shouldn't come off looking like you sidestepped the conflict. It should enable those involved in the conflict to feel that their gripes or complaints will in fact be heard and acted on. The point is to localize the damage, get it out of the meeting setting, give people a chance to cool off, and move the problem to a venue where you're back in charge of the situation. Form a subcommittee; have people go do work; you stay in touch with them while they're working. When their report gets back to the meeting, you'll have had a chance to form a strategy for managing the conflict.

5. You need to establish the size of the issues to be discussed.

The group you're in charge of will have its own particular style of doing business. Groups have personalities: excitable, lethargic, vindictive, uncomfortable. That personality will also determine how they approach discussions. Some groups—through contentiousness or sheer talkativeness—can latch onto almost anything and be ready to chew on it for hours. Others are too polite (or insecure) to be able to get a good discussion going on even the most crucial of issues.

As the group's leader, you're responsible for its efficiency in discussions, and that means your job during the meeting (and when writing the agenda) is to find the most productive scale on which to discuss the items that come up.

Take a group that inflates every issue to the most cosmic level possible: the question of the rudeness of the ushers becomes, say, an unguided tour of sexism in the church, parish personalities, and lots of old business. As chairperson, you'll need to deal with this particular habit; your role will, therefore, often be that of limiting the problem. Quickly, while the group is just getting revved up for a long night of it, you'll have to picture in your mind the appropriate "size" for this issue—a size big enough to deal with the point in question but small enough to mean that a discussion can actually have a beginning, middle, and end (ideally, all within fifteen minutes).

Scaling issues down to a more manageable size, of course, can make it less likely that you'll get a really big change out onto the floor for discussion. Plenty of groups have this problem as well, discussing issues so petty (lector attire, communion traffic) that the net potential effect on their parish's liturgies is incalculably small. "Muddling through" like this has its points: It means you'll avoid major mistakes. Yet your responsibility as chairperson is to break through this level of trivia. If people are griping about the ushers again, it may be productive to talk about the whole issue of hospitality, rather than just picking over the same old hash. Details can be handled by individuals; find issues that are big enough that you need an entire committee to deal with them.

Will you find someone with all these qualifications and skills? If you don't, you can at least choose someone who seems open enough (and a tough enough self-critic) to be willing to work on them. How to manage a meeting while it's happening is a skill you *can* learn through experience. To learn it, though, you at least need to recognize that it *is* a skill—and realize that once the meeting's under way, chairpeople are in fact working constantly, taking the group's temperature and trying to make slight adjustments in the meeting's pace and mood. That means that someone who needs to be everyone's pal may not be a good choice; neither is the person who isn't willing to use a sense of humor to keep everyone loose. Your best candidates may well be the people who simply want to get good at the skill of group leadership—and know that if the group's not producing, the buck stops with them.

The
Agenda

I am a great believer, . . . if you have a meeting, in knowing where you want to come out before you start the meeting. Excuse me if that doesn't sound very democratic.

—Nelson Rockefeller[1]

We've said a lot about agendas in this book, and perhaps we've convinced you already that every meeting—particularly a parish committee meeting—needs an agenda, probably a written one. In this chapter, we'll take a brief look at some sample agendas for both your parish committee and a typical planning group.

THE PARISH COMMITTEE

Perhaps you have an inbred prejudice against the whole idea of an "agenda"—your parish, you may think, is no place for any sort of unnecessary red tape or bureaucracy. *We agree.* We simply think there are some important reasons why a well-crafted agenda can actually be more considerate of your membership, and your parish, than no agenda at all.

1. All in all, parish committees don't meet very often.

It's unlikely that your parish group will be able or willing to meet more than once a month or so, and during the summer you may decide to slow that schedule down even further. That means you have at most *twelve meetings a year* in which to consider some important and complex questions directly affecting your community. If you don't have an agenda—for each meeting, *and* a more general year-long set of priorities for your group—you'll find that the important issues you really mean to talk about somehow fall by the wayside, because you just never seem to have enough time.

1. Quoted in Joseph E. Persico, *The Imperial Rockefeller* (New York: Simon and Schuster, 1982), pp. 209-10.

You *do* have enough time; you just have to plan it well. You can avoid the usual state of affairs by putting together a list of the major issues you want to make sure you deal with *each year*, and then, when planning agendas for individual meetings, making sure that it's *those* issues you're spending the time on, and not simply whatever happens to come up.

This process of formulating the ''big picture'' for your committee shouldn't take an experienced chairperson more than an hour or so of serious thinking each year. Make a list of ten topics you think your committee needs to address; you can consult our list (see ''The Basic Agenda,'' right), or you can use your own judgment about what's important in your parish and what isn't. Now, take that list of topics and pencil in an annual cycle of meetings, assuming that each of those topics is important enough to take up a whole session. What time each year will you review the budget— November? There's one meeting right there. How about a discussion, one year after it started, of your new Saturday evening liturgy? Again, that should probably take up a whole meeting; now you've only got *ten* meetings left, and maybe fewer.

Your time is too precious to waste on unplanned activities, or on whatever axes your members have brought in for their regular grinding. Devote your agenda planning to the big questions; funny thing, you'll find that you won't have room for those silly details that used to take up hours.

2. ● People don't like long meetings.

That's a fact of organizational life, and it's true no matter how much your members like each other and no matter how interesting the discussion is. That's why *no meeting should run longer than an hour*—all right, if you really twist our arms and throw in a coffee break, we'd be willing to go to ninety minutes, but no more than that. You've recruited some busy and talented people for your committee; you have no right to demand that, once a month, they write off an entire evening for your aimless meanderings. People have children to spend time with, television to watch, and other work to do. All those things are more fun than a bad liturgy meeting.

What the One-Hour Rule means, though, is even more pressure on the chairperson to put together a solid agenda shorn of argument and dead air. It also demands that any discussion, even a good and substantive one, be helped along

The Basic Agenda

Parish committees, unlike planning groups, can easily develop a variety of meeting formats: Depending on your group's efficiency and mood, you may decide to have every meeting devoted to a single topic of some importance, instead of trying to jam several important discussions into the same time period. Whatever your preference, however, in the course of a year you'll probably want to touch on a few key topics we've listed below.

You'll recognize many of the concepts from previous chapters, but we hope by listing them again here you'll be even more tempted to place them on your committee's agenda. You'll also note that several of them (like the budget) will call for very specific decisions and recommendations—your meeting on such topics needs to reach closure. Others, like the field trips and the reading projects, are more untraditional, since they will end not with a vote or a decision, but with (we hope) everyone simply having been given something to think about. Perhaps you'll find it useful to alternate one type of meeting with the other, so that if in one month you challenge yourselves with a new point of view or some theoretical background, you can in the next month put that thinking into action through the practical decisions you make on people, money, and parish goals.

1. Overall parish performance. After systematically visiting all the liturgies in your parish at least once a year, you should be able to tackle the issue of overall direction: How would you rate and describe the liturgies in your parish? To which groups does each appeal? Is there enough variety? Too many liturgies? Are your standards high enough? What goal should you set for the following year—can you write one down that sets some specific things you'd like to improve overall? What new liturgical ventures do you want to explore?

continued

67

2. Reactions to individual liturgies. Ask the committee as a whole to attend a liturgy—in your parish, in a neighboring parish, in a church of another denomination. How did you react? What was the overall feeling you got from the liturgy? What would you have changed about it to suit you personally, or to make it a better liturgy?[1]

3. Assessment of planning groups. Does each liturgy at your parish have a functioning planning group? If not, is there anything you can do to recruit such a group, or delegate a group from the parish committee to begin regular planning for that liturgy? Do the groups that *do* exist have anything to report, or any requests they'd like to make from the parish as a whole?

4. Clergy. Are there comments the committee needs to make concerning the clergy who serve the parish? About the system by which they are assigned to liturgies? About the possibility of obtaining the services of outside clergy?

5. Money. How much money is available for liturgy? In what areas could you best make use of additional funds if you had them? Is the money you currently have being allocated in the best possible way? What are the alternatives?

6. Reading projects and guest speakers. Suggest that some or all of your committee members read a book or article, or attend a speech or workshop on liturgy. What did that activity teach you that could have applications to any or all of your liturgies? Did you agree or disagree with the vision of liturgy that seemed to underlie the author's thinking?

7. The liturgical seasons. Does your parish as a whole, and its individual liturgies, reflect the changing moods and themes of the church year? Do your individual planning groups have needs for these seasons (overall parish
continued

---

1. As we'll see in the next chapter, these two issues are completely separate, and it's a good exercise for your group to try constantly to separate the one from the other.

by three important behind-the-scenes activities.

Define exactly what you're supposed to discuss and decide. Don't say that the meeting is "to talk about the budget." Say that, at the meeting, you'll review and select from among several proposals for how your money should be spent. That not only means that you'll save time on talk related to the budget; it means that you have the best excuse in the world for cutting Mrs. Pinkowski short when she begins to wander off on the subject of the Women's Retreat.

The existence of a firm agenda recognizes that big meetings aren't good places for brainstorming or free-form discussion; people need to have a chance to think about the issues at hand *before* they come. That's why it's always a good idea to mail or distribute the final agenda, and as much supporting material as you can get together, to everyone on the committee at least a week before the meeting.

Delegate some initial groundwork beforehand. That meeting on the budget should be preceded—perhaps even several months in advance—by the work of a financial subcommittee on the budget. Its members will get familiar with the parish's current budget and talk informally with the pastor and the various planning groups about what they'd like to see reflected in next year's expenditures. By the time the parish committee's budget meeting rolls around, that subcommittee can present solid alternatives from which the parish committee can set priorities. Particularly if the subcommittee has mailed out some background material to the parish committee *before* the meeting, that means the parish meeting should be over with time to spare.

The same goes for most topics on a parish committee's list. Small groups *do*; big groups accept or reject the judgments of the small groups. The project of, say, evaluating clergy shouldn't begin in a big meeting; it should *end* there, after a smaller group of two or three have already gone through the initial agony of soliciting opinions from planning groups and drafting a short report on the subject that can be submitted to the committee as a whole.

When a discussion isn't making progress, delegate it out for settlement. If, after an hour, none of the budget subcommittee's recommendations have won the group over, and warring factions won't give an inch on where they'd like to see your limited resources spent, you're probably best off giving your group a break and adjourning the meeting. But before you do, ask your poor financial subcommittee to go back to the drawing board and put together some compromise positions.

There are two reasons this helps: First, after an hour, the productivity of your meeting has probably undergone a serious decline anyway; and second, people who have just done a lot of work locking themselves into certain positions on the budget are going to be in no mood to look weak by giving in. When you reconvene next month to look at some fresh proposals, there's a good chance everyone will turn out to be in a much better frame of mind to make a decision quickly.

3. Chairpeople need to know what the meeting is going to be like.

It may be an unpopular thing to suggest, but no unexpected issues should be allowed to come up at a liturgy committee meeting. Unpopular topics, yes; controversial topics, naturally. But nothing that wasn't submitted to the chairperson in writing beforehand, and that he or she did not have a chance to evaluate, discard, rephrase, or delegate to a subcommittee.

The process of making an agenda should certainly include an invitation to the committee as a whole to submit items for inclusion. Yet not every item submitted to a chairperson under this system needs to go on the agenda unedited. Unpopular as this may at times make your chairperson, that job entitles him or her to take unimportant matters (repeated complaints about rubrics), items that aren't the committee's business (certain types of personnel problems), or any type of old business that doesn't need to be reopened, and find another satisfactory resolution *besides* bringing them to the parish committee.

The chairperson has the right to deal with the issue one-on-one with the person who submitted it, or to take it up with a small group of those affected by it—or to turn a trivial observation (on usher behavior) into a larger and more wide-ranging issue (such as whether your parish's liturgies make people feel welcome). The chairperson, if gutsy, can even take a submitted agenda item and throw it away—as long as, in his or her judgment, that course of action will both save the committee time and ultimately prove politically acceptable to the group as a whole.

Above all, what chairpeople have a right to reject is an issue that someone feels needs to be settled—such as the behavior of presiders, the talents of individual ministers or musicians, or liturgical customs—that *really doesn't need to be*

programs, architectural changes, etc.) that will need to be dealt with at the parish level? What feasts will be emphasized in your parish?

8. Your buildings and facilities. How satisfactory are your liturgical spaces for the types of liturgy you want? What do the planning groups say they need? How much would it cost for needed renovations, or facelifts, or lighting and sound systems?

Weekly meetings—often, although not always, for the following Sunday—are the backbone of most planning efforts. Yet like a business that only focusses on the short term, a group that fails to stop regularly and look at the larger picture will ultimately fall short of its goals. Working in a one-week time horizon has several limitations: First, it means you'll rarely be able to undertake a major project—a music or dance performance, say, that requires outside performers and lots of rehearsal. But more critically, you may tend to neglect the profile of feasts and seasons that mark the church year, and in doing so you'll miss a valuable context for understanding and using the readings that underpin your liturgy. If you want to make such seasons special, you'll have to do some background work further in advance.

In parallel with your weekly schedule of meetings, then, should run another process: Several more general discussions each year about the direction of your liturgy, the feasts you (or your parish as a whole) will be emphasizing, and the seasons to which you'll devote special attention. Perhaps you'll simply meet in advance of Lent and Advent, and talk over good ideas you've seen in other churches, or some articles recommended by your pastor or parish committee. In thinking about these seasons as a whole, perhaps you'll discover an overarching message or mood that some consistently applied, season-long liturgical efforts can help develop. Is there a special way we can light the church? Is there a feast that calls for special effort? Is there a significant prayer or rite that should be emphasized each week?

But watch out. Even more than in weekly planning, there is a danger in this process of manufacturing unnecessary or heavy-handed "themes" and concepts; a badly written prayer or an endless song makes no more impact when used on six Sundays of Lent rather than only one. Undemocratic as it may be, your group, if it has the luxury, may

continued

settled. Some issues submitted for your committee's consideration may be things that violate someone's sense of what is proper; that does not imply that your parish committee always needs to rule on such an issue one way or the other. A person or a custom that works quite well for one community may well offend someone else; in such a situation, your committee can decide to go on record condemning the person or custom in question for *all* your parish's liturgies, or it can decide that it's an issue best left up to your individual communities. Good chairpeople know that the latter cases far outnumber the former; that discovery can go a long way in cutting down the number of repetitive agenda items your committee needs to face.

THE PLANNING GROUP

A planning group's meetings need to be just as ruthlessly efficient as your parish committee's. The trouble is, working under the same time constraints, they actually need to *plan liturgies*. But here again, the right approach to the agenda can help.

Unlike the parish committee, which can establish a great deal of variety in the format and topics of its meetings, the planning group will often find itself working with a fixed agenda. Every week, no matter what else it discusses, the group needs to address two important questions: How did things go last week? What do we need to accomplish this coming week? (See "The Big Picture," left.)

Since the group will probably be a smaller one, planning meetings will be more informal than the parish committee, and may even survive without a formal leader. Even so, a basic outline for each week's discussion—as well as a general sense of how much time to devote to each item—will save hours over the course of a year of weekly meetings. Your planning group will, over time, develop a unique style that reflects the personalities and skills of the people involved. If you're just starting up, though, the scenario below may give you some ideas on what to do first. (In addition, since each of its four parts should take no longer than fifteen minutes, it conforms to the all-important One-Hour Rule.)

1. Review

A review of what happened last week is essential. In the case of major goofups and coordination problems, you need to bring them to the attention of those involved; you can't expect people to correct mistakes if they don't even know what went wrong. In the case of special liturgical rites or actions that were meant to accomplish a certain mood or end result, you'll need to share your evaluations about whether you did, in fact, do what you set out to do.

Get the reactions of the *whole group*—this always ruffles feathers, particularly in a group unused to working together, but that should soon cease to be a major obstacle. Remember too that positive evaluations, whether from those involved or those on the sidelines, are just as important as criticism.

Playing a special role in this review process are the honestly represented reactions of members of the congregation. (See "Ask Me No Questions," right.) This means talking to people in an unbiased way (not like one priest of our acquaintance who solicited remarks after liturgy with the greeting, "Wasn't that great?"). When someone in the congregation criticizes one of your decisions, don't respond by trying to justify your choice, or attempting to reason someone into liking something they disliked. Instead, listen and ask questions—what you think you heard someone say the first time may, upon further examination, actually be something quite different.

> Committee Member: Well, Mrs. O'Hara, what did you think of the liturgy today?
>
> Mrs. O'H.: Well, I guess it was OK, but I really don't see how anybody could relate to those organ songs. I just read the missalette until they're over.
>
> Member: What could we do to improve things?
>
> Mrs. O'H.: Get rid of those songs! Find something people can sing.
>
> Member: People aren't singing?
>
> Mrs. O'H.: How could they, when they never heard the song before! And they're too hard to follow, anyway.

The result of two simple follow-up questions? You can now report (correctly) that one member of the congregation says people are unfamiliar with the songs, and that rehearsal or

The Big Picture *continued*

choose to delegate this process of "deep planning" to those members who are most familiar with church traditions, the cycles of readings, and other liturgical resources.

Ask Me No Questions

Perhaps at your planning group's first meeting, someone will have the enlightened idea of taking a parish or community survey on liturgy. Or, more likely, you'll think of a survey when your committee is at loggerheads on some thorny questions it can't resolve. "Let's ask people. That'll settle it."

It probably won't. Let's consider a few guidelines and caveats on surveys.

First: The more concrete the question, the more a survey will do for you. If you want to know how old your parishioners are, where they're from, what masses they go to, how often they attend, and how much money they donate, a survey can give you terrific information. But if you're trying to figure out whether people prefer organ music to guitar music, or whether they *like* your liturgies, then you're in trouble.

The problem is not the idea of asking—it's that questions about people's attitudes are a lot harder to get meaningful answers on. It's rare that a liturgical question can be boiled down to A vs. B; the ones that can ("Would you rather hear a sermon by Father Baker or Monsignor Ferrone?") probably won't get asked.

Let's take the oft-tried question, "Do you
continued

71

prefer organ music or guitar music?'' You can phrase this any number of ways; yet what you're probably measuring is not some sort of general stylistic preference but (a) opinions of *your* organ music and *your* guitar music (or maybe even someone else's); (b) whatever awful thing comes into people's heads when they hear the phrase ''guitar music.'' You're also, of course, neglecting the fact that many people like both—if they're done right.

Even something as simple as ''Do you think the 10:15 liturgy is too long?'' is intertwined with the issue of whether people enjoy being there. If it's a dull liturgy, of course it's too long, and cutting fifteen minutes off the back of it won't make people like it one whit better. Many manufacturers ask prospective customers if their products cost too much, and of course people answer yes—if they don't really want the product in the first place.

It's even tougher to ask more open-ended questions about what people want in a liturgy, or what they think about yours. Just try and find some unloaded descriptive words that mean the same thing to everybody. Do you prefer something prayerful? Spiritual? Moving? Traditional? Instructional? Our answer to that question, like yours, is probably all of the above—or none, depending on *what you mean.*

We're not opposed to gathering information, but make it information that helps you know just who you're planning liturgies for, not something that tries to do the planning for you. If you're doing a survey to settle an argument, or to prevent some needed changes, be advised that it will prove no substitute for planning based on creativity, experience, and just a bit of gambler's instinct.

better leadership in the accompaniment might help. You will avoid reporting (incorrectly) that she hates organ songs. Mrs. O'Hara may be right or wrong—but at least you have a better picture of her reaction than if you hadn't bothered to ask at all.

One final danger when quoting members of the congregation: Accuracy is important. The comments of those who choose to speak with you about the liturgy are not necessarily representative of the assembly as a whole. It would be wrong to report, after speaking with Mrs. O'Hara, that ''Nobody was singing. People can't follow the song.'' Far more correct to take Mrs. O'Hara's observation, report it to the planning group, and file it away in case others like it begin to convince you that you have a serious problem.

This review process doesn't need to be an agonizing soup-to-nuts reevaluation. Set a maximum of fifteen minutes for it and move on.

2. The Readings

Now have some people from your group take the three readings from the Sunday you're concerned with and read them aloud, without anyone following along in a book. Read them in order (the way your congregation will hear them) and don't rush them.

Now skim the immediate reactions of your committee. What hit home? What struck you? What seemed out of place? What had you never heard in that reading before? If the reading bored you, or made you uncomfortable, bring that up, too—that's a valid reaction that may well represent the first feelings of many in your congregation, too.

This is a difficult part of the meeting for a new group—people will think they don't have anything to say. In fact, they do—but they need to get over the feeling that this process is some kind of quiz or (worse) a group-therapy session. What you are trying to do is get at the *mood* of the readings, a mood that will get communicated to the congregation just as strongly as the words do. Are the readings unsettling? Challenging? Comforting? Joyous? Confusing? Are there vivid stories? Do they make you want to celebrate, or sit quietly and think more about how they apply to you?

At this stage, almost any comment is acceptable except one which runs on and on—it's important that nobody hog the show. It's not necessary (in fact, it's downright destructive) to think of this process as one of "finding the theme." (See "Why It's Not a Theme," right.) Instead, simply get one or two very general first impressions from everyone. Somebody should take notes, though, and then—but only then—go on to try to figure out what these readings might have to do with your liturgy.

3. Finding Some Guidelines

Now dig into the words you just heard and ask yourselves: Is there something in these readings that can form the center of that Sunday's liturgy? Are there reactions to those readings that your liturgy could help articulate? What feelings do you think people should come away from your liturgy with?

Here, those members of your group with some background in scripture and theology may want to put their two cents in—knowing the historical background of the readings, as well as what comes both before and after them, often helps make their meaning clear. Here too is the time to refer to any overall planning you have done for a particular liturgical season (see "The Big Picture," page 70); such previous groundwork may mean you can abbreviate this stage of your weekly discussions. Scripture commentaries are also a good idea, as long as you don't become addicted to books that try too hard to "package" the readings into neat, easy-to-digest capsules. But since your "gut" reactions have already been articulated, you shouldn't be too afraid at this stage of consulting the opinions of the "experts."

Yet this is *not* the time to write the homily or pick songs (although the people who will eventually go off and do those things should find this time useful). What you're after here is a more general sense of direction for that particular Sunday. Perhaps what you discover in the readings one week is simply a mood (of celebration, of meditation, of common purpose, of tradition). Perhaps a particular piece of music *will* come to mind, or a poem, or still another reading (scriptural or otherwise). Or, maybe your own community has a pressing need (or faces a nagging challenge) that these readings reemphasize. Not everything that you think of, of course, needs to (or should) find expression in a liturgical action.

Why It's Not a Theme

"When we look at the readings in the planning meeting, aren't we really looking for a theme?" NO. Consider the differences: a theme condenses the readings to some common element, while the planning meeting should multiply alternatives. A theme selects the least common denominator from the readings, and expects that everyone will relate to it; the planning meeting ideally finds a multiplicity of meanings, *some* of which will resonate with *some* of the assembly.

The Advent readings for the Sundays of cycle B in the lectionary provide some good examples of the differences. The first reading of the First Sunday has a wonderfully rich passage from Isaiah (63:16b-17, 19b; 64:2-7). A minimal message or "theme" is that of waiting. But what then of the image of the Father as potter, with us the work of his hands? Or that we are "withered like leaves, and our guilt carries us away like the wind"? Choosing to emphasize these other powerful images—in song or whatever—may not especially underscore the notion of waiting, but may so resonate with the readings themselves as to bring that part of the scriptures truly alive for that liturgy.

4. Some Specifics

Now, finally, take fifteen minutes and see what specific plans could help emphasize or support the message (or messages) you've found in the readings.

Here, unfortunately, the best (and perhaps only) guide is experience going to liturgies, and a familiarity with what the church's tradition of ritual and music has to offer. It helps, for example, to remember that the rite of sprinkling with water, as an occasional replacement for the penitential rite, can both emphasize the symbolism of baptism and set a mood of hopefulness right at the beginning of a liturgy. If that's a message you've discovered in that week's readings, and someone in the group brings up this rite as an idea, now's the time to get out the sacramentary and look over the rite; then, if you decide it's a good option, work out the details of words, logistics, and responsibilities.

Or maybe the readings strike you as seriously challenging ones. Where you use music in such a liturgy, as well as the music's overall mood, should be affected by that reaction. Not that now, at your planning meeting, is the time to sit around and flip through hymnals—but it *is* the point for your music director (he or she *is* at this meeting, right?) to understand that the mood at the opening of the liturgy, as well as during it, could be a bit different from the norm.

There are two pitfalls at this final stage of the process. One is to think of the readings—and of the variables under your control—in exclusively verbal terms. The way to underline the message you've heard in the readings is not to explain them to people in a long introduction to the liturgy, or in endless exegetical notes in the bulletin. What you're after is reinforcing the *feeling* of the readings, not finding other ways to verbalize what the readings have already verbalized better than you can. Think rather of the *other* ways you can communicate[2]—light, pacing, music, even simply the number of people involved in the liturgy.

The second danger is, of course, to feel the need to do *something*. In spite of everything we've said about the importance of planning, you should also feel free to let the readings—and the liturgy—speak for themselves without overtly "special" treatment. Not every set of readings will

2. In the next chapter, we'll analyze these variables, and some others, in more detail.

inspire you; in addition, too many weeks spent attempting too much will ultimately try your congregation's patience as much as total neglect. Much of the power of ritual comes from its repetition, and most of the ritual is already "planned" for you. If you're uninspired on an occasional Sunday, permit yourselves to remain that way.

How
to Talk
about
Liturgy

Now that you have a committee that knows its role, a chairperson who hates wasting time, and a variety of temperaments and viewpoints, you can actually start doing the work for which the rest has only been a prelude: You can start talking about liturgies.

For this process to be successful, however, your group is going to need a common language. That common language shouldn't be a bland one:

> It was beautiful, wasn't it.
> It was a real nice ceremony.
> I loved it.
> I actually cried.

or a combative one:

> That was weird.
> I hate things like that.
> That was completely inappropriate.

but a shared recognition of a few basic liturgical goals, and a common agreement to try to separate personal preference from the issue of good liturgy.

In the first part of this chapter, we'll try to define very briefly what "good liturgy" means, and we'll suggest some exercises your committee may want to work through, either individually or as a group, to help compare your personal likes and dislikes with that standard. In the second part we'll do our best to disassemble a Sunday liturgy, so that in your discussions and planning sessions you'll be better able to see what specific liturgical actions are going into making any liturgy give off the vibrations it actually does.

YOUR SECRET AGENDA

The process of talking about liturgy begins with some serious—and honest—self-examination. Before you open your mouth in a liturgy meeting, criticize anything, or make a single suggestion, there is something you need to realize:

Deep down, there is a way you like liturgy to be.

It may be the way liturgy is in your parish right this moment. It may be some other liturgy you attended at some point in your past. It may be the way you imagine liturgies were like not long after the Council of Trent. It may be particular homilies that have moved you, songs you loved to sing, buildings you are attached to, or even simply the group you were a part of at the time. It may be the fact that you were a participant rather than a spectator. Do you enjoy seeing bishops and cardinals? Do you need to avoid wearing suits and ties?

Think about small details and incidents as well as Big Issues—they count, too. You may think you don't have a model in your head. Sit down, count to thirty, and think carefully—*you do*.

But let's suppose you really can't think of a truly outstanding liturgy that you use as your own internal paragon—well, you have at *least* been to a liturgy that you *haven't* liked. One where a sense of formalism and distance put you off, or one where a phony folksiness communicated itself as disrespect or incompetence. One where boredom and anonymity alienated you, or one where clubbiness and emotionalism nauseated you. Think of the homilies that have offended you, the music you've hated, the buildings that have distracted you with their ugliness. Think back to liturgies you attended when you were very young. What were they like? What do you feel about them now?

Now take these liturgies that come to your mind, good *and* bad, and use five or ten minutes to jot down a few thoughts about them—general feelings as well as specific things you loved or hated. You'll need to imagine these liturgies in some detail, because *the way you feel about any liturgy you'll ever attend is determined to a great extent by its "fit" with those expectations.*

That piece of paper you just finished working on is your secret agenda. It's what you like and feel comfortable with, and what you dislike and would probably work to oppose.

For a genuinely challenging evening, bring in these handwritten jottings and *exchange* them among the members of your parish committee or planning group, and devote a half hour or so to mulling them over. An exercise like that would not only serve to bring out many of the issues that your members are waging clandestine battles over, but it will do one other thing: convince you that you can't *all* be right.

79

AREN'T THERE ANY STANDARDS?

And that's the trouble. You may be tempted to believe—as we all are, on occasion—that the things you like on your written (or unwritten) secret agenda are what constitute *good* liturgy. Not just good, in fact, but right, proper, legal, and useful for others.

As a first step away from this point of view, you may have to slow down and force yourself to admit that everyone—even you—has been at one time or another moved by, and defensive of, something that was objectively "bad." Even when the standards of good and bad can be easily determined by objective criteria (an out-of-tune organ or guitar, for example) there will always be those who find its out-of-tuneness as traditional, familiar, and charming as the incompetence of the person playing it. Bad music, bad architecture, bad reading, and bad customs will always find people to whom they are emotionally important.

Let's say that you, for some reason, were once moved by the children's choir's rendition of "Silent Night." As a liturgy committee member, you have to realize two things. One, it was OK for you to like it, and no one on any liturgy committee has any business telling you that you shouldn't have. You are not necessarily a mental defective, overly emotional, or a bad judge of music. But second, you *do* have to realize that you may rush to the following week's planning meeting ready to book the choir on a national tour only to **find that everyone else on the committee thought it was a hokey arrangement, and sloppily done to boot.** That doesn't mean your reaction wasn't valid, or that the children's choir has to be scrapped. But it does mean that you may need to jot down "children's choir" on your personal list of liturgical issues where you need to recognize your prejudices and emotional involvement—and, on occasion, disqualify yourself from a few discussions.

It is not our intention with this example to suggest that personal preference and emotions are lined up on the one side, and the demands of "quality" on the other. Far from it—your secret-agenda items are not irrelevant, or always wrong. They will be of incalculable benefit to your committee insofar as they motivate you to work for the style and size of liturgy that you want your parish to have. Where your agenda runs into problems is not when it seems to bump into someone else's secret agenda, but when it violates what is, in fact, liturgy's inviolable rule.

ONE RULE AND ONLY ONE

Throughout this book, we have been defending the idea that a wide range of liturgical preferences can and should be accommodated in your community—big communities and small, formal and informal, Mozart and folksong. Now, we're going to suggest that there *is* a unifying standard for all these liturgies, *and it is the only standard next to which they—and your secret agenda—should be constantly compared.* Your parish may develop its own particular style (or styles) of meeting this standard—and you can fight among yourselves about whether you *are* meeting it. What we will not permit you to fight about is the standard itself. That standard is a simple one—and it will be made even simpler if we walk you through it in two stages. The first part is the most important:

1. **Sunday worship is first and foremost a celebration.**

Depending on your background, this may seem obvious to you. If it does, we hope you will bear with us as we try to reconvince you of its importance. If the statement antagonizes you, or at best sounds odd, let's take a moment and see what "celebration" has to do with liturgy.

The first obstacle is that "celebration," of course, is now an official Catholic buzzword, used with abandon at workshops and in liturgical periodicals. Among those in the know, you will find it replacing a number of words formerly used to describe Sunday liturgy: ceremony, mass, worship, even the formerly trendy word "liturgy" itself. What you do on Sunday is still all of those things. But when we say "celebration," we're saying *that* word, and the images it conjures up in your mind, are closer to what Sunday liturgy is supposed to be than the images belonging to any one of those other words.

Well, what *do* you think of when you think of the word "celebration"? Parties? Probably—but what are parties?

People getting together for a purpose: marking a particular turning point and, in a way, giving thanks for it (a new job, retirement, birthdays, New Year's Eve, even just welcoming the weekend). For some of these "parties," there are rituals, words and songs that enable the group to *feel* the occasion, rather than just talk about it in words. What would a birthday be without singing "Happy Birthday," or New Year's Eve without champagne and counting down to midnight?

But perhaps most importantly, celebrations mean that there is more than one person there—a big crowd where you may not know a soul, or a small group of your closest friends. The size and intimacy of the group are less important than the fact that celebration is something people do together, not solo.

So celebration means marking an occasion, with rituals, with other people. Does it also necessarily mean happiness, good times? We think the answer is, primarily, yes.

We are certainly not the first to suggest that the primary response of the Christian to the incredibly good news sent to us in Jesus Christ can only be one of gratitude and *thanks*—and not just a quiet, happy gratitude, but a smile you can't wipe off your face in spite of all sorts of discouragement and affliction. If we all really believed that the news was as good as the gospels say it is, and as we very occasionally experience it in our own lives, then going out to whoop it up is the best possible response, and a response that shouldn't surprise, embarrass, or scandalize anyone.

The fact that most liturgies you have ever been to have been nothing *like* celebrations is too bad, but it does not mean that they *shouldn't* have been. The fact that you really don't feel very much like celebrating on Sunday is also no proof that another liturgy would better express your faith; it only shows that your liturgical community has not made you feel that missing even one Sunday would mean missing a crucial and encouraging time with others, and not simply a mortal sin.

If you don't like the word "celebration," perhaps it's because you suspect that it can easily be used to justify an Up With People glossiness, or a nerdy folk-mass hootenanny that doesn't make anybody feel good. You're right—things like that give celebration a bad name. "Celebration" doesn't imply a particular mood or style that can run on autopilot, or a steady diet of smiles all around (although most American parishes are hardly in danger of lapsing into *that* extreme). People arrive at your liturgies in every sort of state of emotional disruption, and they are entitled to get something out of them no matter what mood they're in.

But you can avoid these pitfalls, and have a far more genuine celebration. That means it's time for us to conclude this topic by going just a bit further, and stop limiting our comparison of "celebration" with birthdays and New Year's Eve. If the closest analogy to "celebration" is the word "party," then remember whenever you think of the word "celebration" that parties aren't always giddy—they can be quiet dinners for two, and they can be uncomfortable family reunions where old wounds are reopened. What *these* celebrations have in common with the happier ones is not the outward trappings of smiles and fireworks, but the fact that they too send you out the door having been forced to see yourself, and your situation, in a different light.

> Consciously or unconsciously, we usually evaluate the goodness or badness of a liturgy by the feelings we have conjured up, whether of reverence, community, solidarity, or whatever . . . . *How should our liturgies be evaluated?* Not by our feelings, but by our actions.[1]

And that's really what we mean when we use the word "celebration"—not balloons and silly hats, but the point that Sunday worship is meant to *affect* you—even *change* you—by bringing you into contact with members of your community for a ritual action. Celebration does not mean emotional manipulation—making you cry during a sappy communion song or smile during a baptism. That kind of reaction is actually all too easy to get—what you're after is *change*. Celebrations are meant to take you out of yourself and your normal setting and routine, pull you up short, bring you into contact with other people, give you food for thought, and get the adrenalin flowing.

Felt that way at a liturgy lately?

2. Sunday worship is first and foremost a celebration. That implies active listening and participation.

If you didn't like the first part of this definition, then it's almost certain that you will like the second even less.

Our claim here runs counter to an opinion you will find regularly in your assembly and your committees. It is often described in more highfallutin terms, but what it boils down

1. Tom Conry, "And Then, The Assembly Responds (The Practice)," *Pastoral Music* 6 (August-September 1982) 27-31. Good reading whenever you're feeling satisfied with yourself.

to is a strong sense that Sunday liturgy is supposed to be an island of spiritual refuge in a disillusioning world. What lies behind such a theory is a very genuine need on the part of all of us for solitude, private prayer, and "religious" surroundings. But to have a genuine celebration, you will have to realize that Sunday liturgy is not primarily intended to address these needs.

Sunday liturgy is not a chance to use music, architecture, and familiar surroundings as your spiritual Sony Walkman, creating the environment you find most conducive to prayer and undisturbed introspection. If you are going to have a successful celebration that genuinely moves and affects people, then your planning is going to have to realize that what distinguishes celebration is that it is both *public* and *communal*. That means the participation of everyone is perhaps your primary goal.

We are not proposing that participation is at all quantifiable. It is all too easy to regard "participation" as sitting closer together, singing louder, or nice comments about the homily after mass. Many of the strategies people employ in an attempt to graft "participation" onto a dead liturgy—a smarmy song leader, for example, bellowing at everyone to "sing out"—neither address the real issue of participation nor do very much to make people feel any more like singing. Clearly, an assembly full of people who do not sing is a matter for concern—but we are more concerned at this point with assemblies who are not even given the opportunity or encouragement to do so. If you buy the concept of celebration, then you also have to buy the idea that every liturgical decision needs to be examined to see if, at every turn, it is being done *to help the assembly feel part of what is going on*, not because it's easy, or already in the book.

Could your liturgy be taking place with a brick wall separating the presider from the assembly, and still feel as if nothing important were missing? Are there no important responses for the assembly to say, no music for them to sing, no words that are addressed to them, no part of the liturgy that seems to *require* their presence? Do the people up there even *look* at the congregation? Perhaps, at one time, the ideal liturgy was one which appeared to be taking place in an almost timeless, idealized state, in which its very regularity, perfection, and other-worldliness were felt to be not only desirable but theologically justified. The principle of celebration does not want to denigrate either private prayer or a sense of continuity and tradition—but it *does* claim that we should not create an atmosphere of sanctity out of a mistaken theory that liturgy is some symbolic something we do for God, at which we are only spectators, meditating on the divine mysteries.

God appreciates our Sunday worship, we're sure, but we doubt he needs it. It is, first and foremost, for *us*. The prayers we say, the music we choose—yes, they are addressed to God. But if they don't represent *our* giving thanks *as a group*—as well as attempt to get *us* moving—they're for naught.

There are other public liturgies of the church well suited to private prayer. But *Sunday* liturgy, says the principle of celebration, has as its unique and special function the celebration of the church *as community*. If you really want privacy, you can visit the church building when it's empty—a revival of this custom would be an admirable thing. If you want to think deeply while listening to music, go to a concert—the music on Sunday is generally to be sung along with, not to be used as background music or for scholarly research. If you want nice warm feelings, have a dinner party—the celebration at Sunday liturgy isn't just to make you feel good.

Perhaps you have reservations about participation based on a suspicion that participation means breaking ''the rules.'' Maybe it will make you feel better if we claim that participation does not mean dreaming up all sort of new prayers, sugary announcements, and oddball rites. It *does* mean more than just reading what's in the official books; it means imaginatively making use of the opportunities the books offer for building a sense of celebration. The only rules celebration requires you to break are unwritten ones: about how churches are supposed to be decorated, about establishing human contact and conversation before, during, and after a liturgy, about attention being paid to usually neglected parts of the liturgy, and about whether you should leave a Sunday liturgy happy, or just quickly.

THE LITURGICAL BUILDING BLOCKS

L et's suppose you've all agreed on such a goal for your liturgies—unlikely, but let's suppose it. Your committee then has only one topic left to discuss—whether the liturgy you just attended met that goal or not, and if it

As examples of the kind of critical eye we're trying to encourage in this chapter, let's take a quick look at ten common liturgical practices. Small though they are, we think they all do quite a bit to fight the important process of building a sense of celebration and participation.

What we hope they help you realize is that in liturgy, *everything* communicates. Even little actions and omissions that you have long taken for granted are telling your assembly about your theology, your priorities, or your carelessness.

1. Bells.

The little bells you ring after the hosanna, and twice during the elevations—why are you doing it? If it is to call attention to the sanctity of the moment, you could do it more effectively by more subtle, yet more powerful means—slowing the pace, silence, a sense of respect and concentration on the words being said.

2. Altar boys (and girls, too).

Altar servers have no real function in most liturgies—they don't have any lines, they are not some sort of symbolic "representatives" of the assembly, and if you stop to think about it they really don't have to hold books, move candles, or help Father wash his hands. You need no unnecessary people around the altar—and certainly not remnants of what is now a sexist custom maintained only because of its imagined role as a vocation factory.

3. Altar rails.

You don't need a barrier to keep people from going into the area around the altar—there's nothing up there they can't touch or walk on. A rail says that what happens up there is for looking at, not for becoming a part of. (See the guidelines in *Environment and Art in Catholic Worship* by the American bishops; the bibliographic reference is in the Appendix.)

continued

didn't, *what you can do about it*.

The process by which you can translate theory into practice is, in a way, what we have so far encouraged you *not* to do: trade in the big picture for the little picture, and dissect your liturgy to examine all the smaller parts it was made of. The spiritual power of a good liturgy is only partly a miracle; it is also the careful product of lots of hard work and good judgment, and dozens of individual decisions on a a variety of details. Some of these "details," like the space you worship in and the presiders you have, are really too big to be called details; but on the other hand, neither should you be too quick to dismiss them as "givens" over which you have no control.

With that in mind, here is a list of variables you may want to consider when attending a particular liturgy for the first time, or when you need to take a few steps back and evaluate a liturgy you normally attend or plan. All the liturgical building blocks in the list below *are* under your control, and the care with which you work with them will be what determines the ultimate fate of your liturgies.

1. Space

What did the space feel like when you walked in?
Was the liturgy in the most appropriate space available?
What effect did the seating arrangements have?
Was there a good enough sound system and lighting setup?
Was lighting used creatively?

When you enter an unfamiliar place for a Sunday liturgy, do you form an immediate impression of what that liturgy is going to be like?

We do—and we suspect that everybody somehow picks up messages from all the powerful architectural and aesthetic "signals" provided by your building and its fixtures. You are, quite literally, *surrounded* by your surroundings, and it is necessary to be sensitive to exactly what each detail is communicating. Size, layout, sound and light are so powerful that all your best efforts in other areas may not be able to counteract bad judgment in their use.

Size. There *is* an ideal size for a worship space: Big enough for the people worshiping in it, but no bigger. This, of course, probably helps you not at all. Perhaps the problem is overcrowding—you're not likely to have the money to make a big church even bigger. Or, perhaps your building is far too large for the congregations that use it—the only way to make it smaller, after all, is to start over (or, of course, renovate a smaller space you could use for smaller Sunday and weekday liturgies).

The point, though, is that you should at least check to see if a liturgy is taking place in the best place you have available for it. A sparse crowd in a big church space will, like a gas, expand to fill the container provided; most Catholics don't come to church expecting human contact, and they will take up positions that "defend" them against such unwanted intrusion. By suggesting that you may want to develop a smaller space for small groups, we're not suggesting that you corral people into somewhere they don't want to be; we *are* suggesting that wide-open spaces are the enemy of participation and celebration. Take a hard look now and then at how well your space needs match up with the number of people you actually have.

Layout. Just as important as finding the right *size* space is the issue of how people find themselves seated. People need to be able to see what they are participating in—and what they need to see is not only the priest and the altar, but the other people they are there with.

Seating arrangements imply roles: Where do people sit in rows, all facing forward? In a concert hall or movie theater. Does that mean participation? No—it means you shut up, talk in whispers if you talk at all, and try to ignore the person next to you. We hope it is not inappropriate to suggest that a dining room, rather than a theater, is the model you should set up in your minds for Sunday liturgy: people seated around a table, rather than people waiting for a show to begin.

Ugly and foolish as many people are, in liturgy they are not only *not* a distraction but an important symbol of what you are there to celebrate. Yes, in the long term the best course might well be a rather substantial and expensive reorganization of your church, a rearrangement that guarantees that everyone can see the face (or the profile) of at least some other people in attendance, and feel as though the altar and lectern are not set apart from them as on a stage or pedestal. Will you need to rip out your pews, move the altar forward, and arrange seating in a semi-circle or U-shape around the altar? That's for you and a good architect to decide, but it may well be the case, and it may even mean you have to spend some money. If so, spend enough to have the job done right—it may be the best investment you ever make, because you will be making a strong and permanent statement about what is actually going on in your parish on Sundays.

Audio. Just a word to point out that this is America in

Quick Fixes *continued*

4. Secular greetings.

"Good morning." "Good morning, Father." "In the name of the Father, and the Son, and the . . ." How many beginnings do you need? Liturgy is hard enough to start properly without doing it over and over.

5. Themes.

"The theme of today's readings speaks to us about . . ." Readings don't have themes, they have messages, and even the most powerful messages can't help but sound trite when someone tries to boil them down into an easy-to-remember concept.

6. Visitors from outer space.

You know what we mean. Homilists who suddenly appear from a side door, and disappear right after the homily. Eucharistic ministers (or, more likely, extra clergy) who loiter in the sacristy and make an ill-timed appearance just in time to help with communion. The liturgy has no guest stars; its positions of leadership and service should be taken only by those who have been part of the assembly for the whole celebration.

7. Genuflecting to nothing.

Genuflecting to the eucharist, particularly when it is reserved in a tabernacle, is a common practice. But many people, particularly ushers, do it every time they pass in front of an altar, even though the tabernacle got moved from behind the altar a long time ago. The altar, the sanctuary, and the presider do not require you to assume this position; doing it means that these things acquire an aura they neither deserve nor need.

8. Talking too fast.

Most words in a liturgy get spoken too quickly; mumbling and rushing means what you're saying isn't important. Better to have fewer words than say stuff you're just rushing through to get it over with.

continued

9. Second collections.

It's hard enough to find a way to take up a collection that doesn't stop a liturgy dead in its tracks; squeezing in another one, either right after the first one or after communion, is surely over-emphasizing a subsidiary purpose of the mass. Isn't there another way to raise even more money and not interrupt the liturgy—direct mail, phone campaigns, more bingo?

10. People who close their eyes.

Presiders, musicians, and others who feel that such moments as the consecration require total isolation are making the moment seem more like one of magic than faith. They are also inviting a number of reasonably amusing practical jokes to be played on them while their eyes are shut.

the 1980s, and the art of sound reproduction has made remarkable advances. You do not have to settle for a sound system that fails to make what happens in the front of your church audible *and* natural-sounding to a person even in the last row.

Step back and listen to your old P.A. system every year or so—*during an actual liturgy.* Is its signal lost in reverberation? Do voices *sound* electronic and amplified? Do things get too loud? Too soft? Are you using a P.A. system in a small space where you really don't need one? Do your goose-neck microphone stands creak whenever anyone steps up to the lectern and makes the mistake of adjusting one of them? Do you have dusty switches that CRACK into place at top volume when someone turns on a mike? Do you have *enough* mikes, and enough flexibility to give a group of guitarists and singers all the mikes they need, adjusted at proper levels? Does someone monitor and have control over how things sound *during* each liturgy?

Yes, we're talking about more money here, and the need to search out a genuine sound expert rather than Mr. O'Malley, your local electrician, who would be delighted to sell you a big order of speakers and amplifiers—at, of course, a generous clerical discount. Good sound is one of the few major capital investments you need to make for good liturgy, and how subtly and smoothly the system works can make the difference between someone listening to the readings—or looking distractedly out the window.

Lighting. While on the subject of capital investment, remember that while a church doesn't need to have the lighting flexibility of a Broadway theater, lighting *is* an important tool in which even the most ancient liturgical traditions require variety. Even for the simplest liturgies and buildings, it's invaluable to have a lighting system that is more than the customary on-off variety. (''On,'' in most churches we've seen, is using the term loosely.)

Lighting is a variable like words and music: It speaks powerfully of the mood you're trying to create, and focusses attention where it ought to be at a particular time. On the feast of Christ the King, your church may be ablaze with lights and candles. On the First Sunday of Advent, you may have only the sanctuary lit, in a darker, warmer glow—the contrast, on these two consecutive Sundays, will be striking enough to require no wordy explanation of the change in seasons. Find someone in your town who has some experience in theatrical lighting, and who also recognizes the moods and rites of the liturgical seasons and feasts; ask for some specific advice about what you need. It will be money well spent. (Again, watch out for Mr. O'Malley.)

2. The priest

Did the presider set a mood and pace that welcomed people and encouraged celebration?

How was the homily?

We've said before that a presider can make or break a liturgy. Your diagnoses of sad liturgical cases may well end right here: No liturgy can survive a presider who is uninvolved with the liturgy and its community or, even worse, terminally bad at what is admittedly his very difficult job. (See "Tips from the Clock," right.)

Presiding style. Part of this power to make or break comes not simply from his skill at writing and delivering homilies but from how well he fulfills the more personal requirements of his official role. That role is not to be the priest, or even the "celebrant" (you are celebrating, too). The priest at a liturgy is there to *preside*. Master of ceremonies? A bad pun, but perhaps accurate: At Sunday worship, a priest sets the mood and the pace, and serves as leader of the community's prayer.

When this is well done the role itself is transparent, and you see an individual personality, not someone reading official things from books. Your impression is one of naturalness, and a sense that the presider is both comfortable and—imagine it!—*happy* to be there.[2] This gets communicated not by smiling all the time (revolutionary as that would be), or by a schizoid alternation between a rushed, official tone and talkative folksiness, but by a sense of both ease and leadership.

Do your presiders make good eye contact? Or do they look at the books too much? Do their gestures seem like uncomfortable poses, or like natural extensions of the words they're speaking at the time? Do they rush? Do they shout? Do they *vary* speeds? Are they uncomfortable or perfunctory in those parts of the mass not written down verbatim in the book? Do they sing when the assembly is supposed to be singing (or is that when they look around uncomfortably, waiting for it to be over)? Your only hope may be that in such specific details there are things that a strong planning group can help your presiders to correct, one by one.

2. For a more in-depth description of the presider's role, see Robert W. Hovda's *Strong, Loving and Wise* (Collegeville: The Liturgical Press, 1976).

Never underestimate the value of feedback—priests do not get very much of it, aside from the perfunctory comments about the homily on the church steps. If you have a regular priest and a regular planning group, you are in a good position to swallow hard and begin to point out the areas in which your presider could use some improvement—they may be things he is clearly opposed to or incompetent at, but on the other hand they may simply be details he has never thought about before. Such a process does not need to be a hostile one, as long as those involved have the tact and good will necessary to provide constructive feedback.

Homilies. What your planning group *can't* do, however, is write homilies. You can torture yourself by reading books of outstanding homilies[3], and you can try to isolate the features that make up a good one: brevity and organization; power, and a call for change; eloquence; a sense that the preacher knows your deepest concerns, fears, and self-destructive habits; an absence of trite examples and tiresome doctrinal defenses; a reliance on the readings for themes and ideas. However you would describe a great homily, though, the characteristics of a bad one are equally numerous—occasionally funny, but usually just painfully annoying. A homily is often the longest uninterrupted liturgical action in any given celebration; you can never overestimate the overall effect a rotten one can have on how you reacted to a liturgy.

Again, if faced with a mumbler or a droner, do not underestimate the power of honest, regular, fair feedback. You are entitled to give it, and homilists need to hear it. Be specific and constructive: What would be a useful time limit? Should your presider start attending your planning meetings to get a better sense of how the scripture readings have affected the mood of the rest of the liturgy?

In the worst case, of course, a serious lack of skill or a loud defense of clerical prerogatives cannot be overcome by corrective comments. As a last resort, don't overlook a long-term lobbying effort (and a commitment of parish funds) for the purposes of importing an occasional desirable presider or homilist from a local school, college, hospital or monastery. Heaven knows that the shortage of clergy makes such an arrangement difficult, but *it can be done.* Whatever your strategy, however, do not be ashamed to make your opinions on this crucial variable known.

3. Although they lose something without the benefit of his skill at delivering them, you could try the homilies in Walter J. Burghardt, S.J.'s *Tell the Next Generation* (New York: Paulist, 1980), *Sir, We Would Like to See Jesus* (New York: Paulist, 1982), and *Still Proclaiming Your Wonders* (New York: Paulist, 1984).

3. Music

Did the music make you feel like singing?
Were the musicians performing, or leading? Were they
musically competent?
Did the selections reinforce or conflict with the overall mood
of the liturgy and readings?
Why was there music at any given point?

As we've said throughout this book, picking music is your musicians' business, and disputes about Song A vs. Song B are far too trivial for a parish committee's attention. Nevertheless, planning groups and parish committees are going to need to evaluate music *and* musicians periodically—and we hope these brief comments help you go beyond the usual skirmishes about likes and dislikes.

Music gets everyone riled up in liturgy committees in part because there are, as we write, no ''official'' musical styles or compositions for the church (in spite of what some of your members would like you to believe). The reason you use music in your liturgies is not simply because you're supposed to, but because it is one of the most powerful tools at your disposal to make a liturgy work better. The evaluation of the music or musicians at any liturgy is much more properly oriented around not what songs they sang, or what instruments they played, but *whether they helped the congregation celebrate and participate.*

How do you know if music is doing that? One way—although it's a terribly subjective and inexact one—would be to ask yourself if the music actually made things seem to go *faster*, rather than making the liturgy drag (as many parishioners still complain). Music has that effect of speeding things up when its planners have ensured that it is not simply used as an interlude to fill time until the next ''important'' part of the liturgy, or as an indulgent lingering on old favorites, but *a way of enabling people to feel more deeply what any particular liturgical action is all about.*

Take the beginning of the liturgy: it demands a spirit of community, gathering, and (usually) festivity. An opening song should, by its selection and performance, support and even help build that mood. Songs that fail to do this (through unsingability, poor warmup of the congregation, or bad performance) are pointless, and you'll feel—*rightly*—as though you were wasting your breath doing something you weren't enjoying. You need a real ''lift'' from an opening song, and that's hard to get—but evaluate the music that opens your liturgy based on whether it succeeded in giving that "lift," not primarily on whether you liked the words, or whether it was an organ song or a guitar song, or whether you like other songs better. Those are all subsidiary to the issue of whether the music did what it needed to do.

Or take the gloria—due to its length and meter, it's usually considered a difficult part of the liturgy to deal with musically. Yet the guidelines for evaluating its musical treatment are fairly simple, if often violated. The gloria is a prayer of praise; that implies two things. First, it belongs to the assembly: If you decide to use music to emphasize the gloria it ought to be a musical setting that the congregation has some part in. (Better to leave the gloria out entirely than turn your assembly into an audience.) And second, your musical setting had darn well better end up sounding like praise, or it's not worth doing. Don't sing the gloria because you think it would be nice; sing it because by singing you can make it have more of the effect it was meant to.

What all this boils down to is three rather simple observations on evaluating music:

1. In general, liturgical music "works" when it supports the overall mood of a particular celebration.[4] Someone who's great at finding songs wherein there is a clever tie-in in the fourth verse with a line from that Sunday's second reading is less valuable to you than someone who can find the song that creates the right *feeling* at a particular liturgical juncture. Words matter, but not as much as emotional rightness.

2. But words do matter. They matter not so much because of clever tie-ins which no one picks up on at the time, but because the words you're singing can have a subtle, subliminal clash with what's supposed to be going on. Read through the words of songs and ask yourself whether it at least makes *some* sense to be singing this today, on this feast, with these readings. Watch out for things that sound stilted, or just plain silly:

> Sent forth by God's blessing,
> Our true faith confessing,
> The people of God from his dwelling take leave.

---

4. For an excellent application of this idea of "mood" to the work of the weekly planning group, see Robert Dufford, S.J., "St. Louis Jesuits Plan Liturgies around Mood and Feeling," *Hosanna!* 3 (December 1977) 14-16.

(Why sing to describe what you're doing at the time? And besides, you aren't leaving yet.) And also double-check the words of even those songs which have just the mood you want; in the bright, upbeat "Blest Be the Lord," you'll find

> I'll not be shaken with the Lord at hand.
> His faithful love is all the armor that I need
> To wage my battle with the foe.[5]

We hope that rules it out for most weddings.

3. Before you worry at all about specific musical selections, however, take an even harder look at *where* you use music in a liturgy, rather than *what*. The four-hymn mentality (entrance, offertory, communion, closing) makes for easy planning; it also neglects, among other things, the priority of the psalm as a part of the liturgy that should be *sung*, not read in unison.[6] It also means that you may neglect the possibilities offered by opening and closing in silence on occasion, and risk emphasizing parts of the liturgy (such as the preparation of the gifts) that really don't need singing for any better reason than to kill time during the collection. Examine where you sang in a liturgy based on where singing was liturgically sensible, not where you wanted music to fill some imagined hole.

Now, after you've put your thoughts together on whether the music was well chosen and structured, you can evaluate the *performance* of the musicians as *a separate issue*. And while good musicians' virtues are many and complex, perhaps it's simpler for our purposes to raise the spectre of their primary vice: self-indulgence. You'll find self-indulgence lurking in two common forms:

1. A love of performance. The welcome rise of professionalism in church music does not mean that churches are now concert halls or night clubs. The more professional and well-trained the musician, however, the greater the temptation to let musical considerations outweigh the demands of celebration. There are music directors who have professional choirs sing important congregational parts of the mass, and even ask the assembly to sit down during them to relax and listen. Similarly, brilliant organists can play too

5. From *Songs of the Saint Louis Jesuits*, comprehensive edition (Phoenix: North American Liturgy Resources, 1978).

6. For more specific guidance about what parts of the liturgy take musical priority, see the Catholic bishops' statement on *Music in Catholic Worship* (see Appendix).

quickly, too slowly, or with too little attention to giving people an audible melody line; and cantors with operatic training often do a lot more to encourage passive listening than provide a role model for those who are normally a bit tentative about joining in.

Good pastoral musicians are always good musicians, but they also know that liturgical music has a special role, and that what they are doing is encouraging participation and prayer as much as providing great art or fun entertainment.

2. Being blind to incompetence. People do not sing along with, enjoy, or appreciate untrained, sloppy, amateurish organists, singers, or guitarists. Period. That means, in spite of what you may believe, that having *something* in the way of music is not necessarily better than having nothing. Music at Sunday liturgy is happily now considered normative. But that fact does not justify the continued employment of anyone whose contribution to a sense of celebration is, in the balance, a consistently negative one.

Obviously, except in extreme (and probably amusing) cases, opinions on such a topic will differ; some people are far more snooty in their standards than others, and that's unavoidable. But, before deciding that the incompetence of the person doing the music was responsible for your not liking a liturgy, make *sure* you are not confusing musical competence with the issue of songs you don't like, music that's badly chosen, composers you detest, and styles or periods of music you are just never comfortable with. The issue of whether the music was appropriate *for that liturgy* is separable from the issue of whether it was competently done.

4. ● Visual Impact

Did the important liturgical symbols make the impact they needed to?

This is a hard section to put into words, for it calls upon some exclusively nonverbal skills that are often those most lacking in a liturgical planning group: those, essentially, of the dramatist.

What we are trying to get across with the concept of "visual impact" is that certain liturgical symbols, actions, and objects are more important than others; you can reinforce their importance by making sure that they *look* important. What happens at your liturgy should be as clear and fully experienced by a deaf person as by anyone else there; liturgies which depend too much on words to get their points across are in the long run less powerful than those which are also able to use the tools of gesture, movement, dance, and, most importantly for our purposes here, *symbol*.

Altar. Cup and plate. Lectionary. Crucifix. Two candles. The physical objects which first come to mind when you think of Sunday liturgy are the ones which, upon walking into a church, should grab your attention—through how they are lit, how big they are, and how good a job people have done in peeling away needless distractions. The altar, the presider's chair, and the lectern are, for example, really the only three areas people need to see during a liturgy; a liturgical space with ornate side altars, racks of votive lights, statues and flower vases, scriptural banners, a manger scene, and a tabernacle dead center in the sanctuary is doing its subtle part to prevent people from focussing on what are, in the main, simple and powerful symbols and shapes. This is not to criticize baroque architecture or historic buildings—far from it. It is only to say that when you walk into a liturgical space what should dominate your attention is not the complexity of the space but its essential simplicity.

Visual impact is not only created by major forces like architecture. There are dozens of bad little habits which do their part to rob liturgical symbols of their power to communicate. An altar is an altar, not a desk; a pile of different books, a mike, six chalices, Father's glasses, the cruets, and two copies of the announcements distract people's attention from the bread and wine. Similarly, does the cup you use look like a real cup? Does what you use to hold the bread look like another cup, or like a plate or a bowl *meant* for bread? Eucharistic minsisters are invaluable symbols of service to the assembly—but do you have so many ministers, lectors, and altar servers coming and going in the sanctuary that the roles of presider and lector are robbed of their power? You don't need to go out and strip churches bare, like Cranmer; but it wouldn't hurt to insure that everything up in the sanctuary really needs to be there (also see "The Paper Chase," right), and that the important objects used in liturgy are permitted to look like what they are.

The Paper Chase

The same rule—if it's not necessary, get rid of it—goes for all the paper a congregation usually has to deal with while it's seated in the pews.

People need to be able to read about what's going on in a liturgy only insofar as it assists their spoken and musical response. That means that while music, words to hymns, and prayers other than the standard ones should of course be made available, anything else is only a distraction that works to reinforce a passive role. This rather nasty statement includes, in its condemnation, your diocesan newspaper, your bulletin, prayer cards, and bibles; useful as these publications are, they are for afterwards, not for *during* liturgy. Most especially, we mean to exclude missalettes, which are to most liturgies what programs are to concerts: something to read for those who are just a bit bored with what's going on.

You can put together a worship aid—preferably a songsheet or other bulletin custom-made each week for a specific liturgy—to give people the music they need to participate. Anything else, particularly if it reproduces that Sunday's readings, damages many of your liturgical efforts but none so completely as the impact of hearing scripture proclaimed. Those readings are to be listened to, not read along with; missalettes and hymnals that enable people to follow along rob the readings of the power they have even with the worst of lectors. When people don't have the words in front of them, they actually need to listen; if they can follow along, it's often the case that the *process* of following along is itself absorbing enough to let the words go in one ear and out the other. The role of the lector becomes superfluous, and the care and preparation that goes into an excellent job of lectoring is drowned out by a wave of communal page-turning.

If you're concerned about people not being able to hear the readings, first pay attention to the P.A. system and your lector training program; if you have people in your assembly who are hard of hearing, we're sure you can

continued

make some arrangements for them to have copies of the readings available for their personal use.

Watch Your Mouth

Often lost amidst skirmishes concerning *musical* selections is the equally important question of what you *say*. We think you have probably noticed in your liturgical travels that an over-reliance on words does serious damage to the liturgy—particularly if you have a presider who thinks every ritual and nonverbal event needs a verbal introduction ("These palms we are going to carry today are what we call 'symbols' . . ."). But this is not to excuse you from exercising great care in the words you *do* use.

Words, like music, communicate. Prayers from the sacramentary can go in one ear and out the other, or (depending on your editing work[1] or how well they are delivered) they can pull you up short with their power and imagery. Male-dominated language may not bother *you* much, but it can ruin a liturgy for those sensitive to it—and those people are entitled to be offended by your thoughtlessness in continuing to use it. Even something as pedestrian as your parish announcements can make upcoming events sound like fun, or as dull as the person who wrote the announcements.

You can at *least* pay some attention to the one part of the liturgy that *demands* your

continued

1. Books with some outstanding presider's prayers (and ideas for prayers of the faithful) include Huub Oosterhuis' *Your Word Is Near* (New York: Paulist, 1968) and John Mossi, S.J.'s *Bread Blessed and Broken* (New York: Paulist, 1974).

5. Pacing

Did the liturgy have a center? Did you come away from it having remembered any particular part?

How you set the *rhythm* of a liturgy, like how you control its visual imagery, also plays a part in determining its power as a ritual action. If you don't understand quite what we mean, it might be fun sometime for you to take a few sheets of graph paper, and try to chart a liturgy you just attended on both (a) your general sense of its flow and (b) how important various parts of it were made to seem to you.

If you don't get any signs of life on this liturgical EKG, then something's wrong. Liturgies which run through the readings and prayers at a steady clip, and don't stop to pay attention to any of its parts, are celebrating liturgy the way a computer might perform Beethoven's Ninth: The notes are all there, but the lack of interpretive insight robs the music of its power.

What do you emphasize in a liturgy? From week to week, that's up to your planning groups—all we're asking you to remember at this stage is that *it is a variable under your control*. How much time you allot to certain parts of the liturgy, and how you set them off through the subtle use of pacing, light, silence and music, determines whether they grab people's attention or just whiz by. Remember too that when you emphasize something, you will need to deemphasize something else, lest you again be caught with everything in your liturgy making the same bland impression of roteness.

To take just one example, many good liturgies successfully emphasize the gathering, the readings, the homily, and the eucharistic prayer simply through ensuring that the parts of the liturgy in between these elements are dispatched with the greatest possible simplicity and lack of delay and bumbling. In this scenario the readings, surrounded by carefully maintained periods of silence and read with deliberateness and power, can have a chance to stand out; such emphasis is not often gained through simply verbal means ("Now listen very carefully to the first reading today, and imagine you're hearing it for the *first time . . .*"). (See "Watch Your Mouth," left.) Such an effort, however, will also require a deemphasis on, say, the often endless period between the end of the prayers of the faithful and the preface. Clogged with a collection, a song, a procession, prayers over the gifts, and lots of dead time with people sitting around waiting, this period can instead be got through quickly in a swift, well-coordinated effort to get all that done with before people even know what's hit them. By occasionally stressing one part of the liturgy, you do not denigrate another.

In liturgy, departures from the norm grab people's attention; by carefully regulating the way your liturgy ebbs and flows, you can use this fact for constructive purposes, and not simply annoying ones.

6. A Sense of Occasion

Did you feel welcome, and happy to be there?

Most good liturgical communities spend an awful lot of time talking about making people feel welcome. What they are after might best be described as a sense of occasion.

Such issues are often too quickly lumped together under the heading of "hospitality," and palmed off on the poor ushers and the coffee committee. Yet having someone at the door of the church, smiling and handing out song sheets as people come in, is only one step toward creating a real sense of occasion. Whether people feel welcome, excited, and happy to be there when they walk into your church, and eager to stay around after they leave, has very little to do with whether you even *have* ushers. Instead, you might look at what sort of behavior your worship space is silently encouraging as soon as people walk in the door—because that's when the liturgy begins, not when Father crosses himself.

Is your presider in the church, carrying on conversations with people? How about the musicians and the other ministers—is anyone in evidence at all? Are they seated quietly whispering to each other, or freely carrying on conversations with their colleagues and friends in the assembly? Is there music playing which is telling people to be quiet? Or is there a hubbub of conversations and greetings as people come in and find seats next to their friends and neighbors? All these things may seem to you to be breaking (unwritten) rules concerning pre-mass behavior; a required thirty seconds of kneeling upon entering may well be more familiar to you as the accepted way to get fired up for a Sunday celebration. Unfortunately, a liturgy that begins from a silent, cold start is almost impossible to get

creativity with words: the prayers of the faithful. Note that the title says prayers of the *faithful,* not the prayers of the homily-helps service, or of the guy who wrote the canned prayers of the faithful. This part of the liturgy is intended for *your* assembly's concerns and hopes, not another part of the liturgy done straight from the book, or (worse) a recap of the homily. Need help? In a perceptive little book on liturgy,[2] Bishop Kenneth J. Untener has put his finger on one secret of writing good prayers of the faithful: avoidance of the "that" clause. It's enough, he writes, to pray for the poor, and not for the poor *that they may find jobs and reconciliation with all members of God's holy people.*

Put some effort into this part of the liturgy—consider, if you have a small congregation, taking a few minutes each Sunday and asking for your assembly's prayers from the pews. At the very least, have someone in every planning group assigned to the task of writing prayers each week, and ask for them to be simple, to-the-point, eloquent, and above all, custom-made.

2. *Sunday Liturgy* Can *Be Better* (Cincinnati: St. Anthony Messenger Press, 1980), pp. 70-71.

moving in time for the opening song; if you want your church quiet when you walk in, then you'd better realize that there are inevitable trade-offs in terms of how welcome and enthusiastic people will feel, not only when they walk in the door, but throughout the entire liturgy.

In some genuinely vital liturgical communities, the mood before a celebration begins is not unlike backstage before the curtain goes up. If you want your community to feel like that, it will take time; to do it, you will need to make friendly behavior, conversation, and introductions all around seem like the norm rather than the exception. When you succeed, you will also find that a great beginning to a liturgy (see "The Right Foot," right) exerts a powerful push that can carry a sense of participation all the way through to the end. Even your traditional rush to the parking lot when the liturgy is over may well slow to a far more pleasant pace.

The Right Foot

Shuffling feet, coughs, silence. A lector walks to the microphone and clears his throat. "Good-morning-everyone-and-welcome-to-St.-Athanasius's. [Long pause. Examines papers.] Let us stand and greet our celebrant as we sing "Hail, Holy Queen . . ."

Not an auspicious beginning. Let's leave aside the fact that the purpose of singing at the beginning of a liturgy is not to greet the celebrant. What's more important is that this way of starting a liturgy is trying to get a heavy freight train—your assembly—into high gear with no period for acceleration.

If you're on a planning group and you'd like to improve your liturgies, you'd do well to take a year or so and simply perfect how you begin it—not the opening song, but what happens before the opening song even sounds its first note. That crucial period is often made even more dull with endless rehearsals, analyses of the "theme" of the liturgy, and silence waiting for something to happen; savvy parishioners know to arrive late and avoid such dead air. Instead, during that period you need not only to get people *musically* prepared to sing, but happy and ready to celebrate with people who do not feel like strangers. A few suggestions:[1]

1. Rehearsals should be short and concise—their purpose is not to teach people every note, but simply to get them warmed up, and used to the idea of singing. Make it fun.

2. Particularly in urban churches, people may well need to be introduced to each other, *every week*. Ask them to say hello to the person seated next to them, or to tell each other where they were born. Some people will hate it—at first.

3. Consider having the presider in place throughout the musical preparation. If he's participating, people may be more inclined to take it seriously—and, perhaps, to show up on time. You can then have a few moments of silence after the rehearsal to separate that part of your preparation from the gathering song.

1. We are indebted here to Elaine Rendler's excellent article, "First, the Assembly Gathers (The Practice)," *Pastoral Music* 6 (August-September 1982) 15-17.

APPENDIX

Self-Help

To many liturgy committee members, "education" will seem like a boring word, as will "reference" and "resource." Nevertheless, if your committee is going to keep liturgies moving and its level of interest high, you're going to need occasional inspiration and information from the outside world.

A BASIC LIBRARY

T he books below are *basic* in both senses of the word: they're easy to read, *and* they're a starter set that will help provide a firm foundation for your group's discussions. They are also generally easy to find and reasonably priced, and we hope you decide to make the whole list required reading for your group.

Why "required"? Because having a few books that *everyone* on your committee has read will give you some touchstones and authorities to refer to during your deliberations. They will help develop a sense that the liturgy as it exists in your parish is by no means the way liturgy has always been, needs to be, or should be—and that the problems you face are not unique ones. Between them, they'll provide you with a bit of history, some theology, all the readings, lots of tips and suggestions, most of the liturgical rules and regulations, and a passing acquaintance with some of the interesting and opinionated people currently writing on liturgy. (Naturally, we mostly agree with those opinions—that's why these books are in the list.)

Our selection is not at all scholarly, and very incomplete. You will look in vain for books on a whole range of other topics in which you or one of your members may develop an interest: drama, ritual, music, liturgical history, architecture, liturgy in other religions and denominations. A member who decides to become the resident expert (or bore) on these subjects will find a lifetime of reading available. Everyone, though, should establish the following as common ground.

YOUR TWO BIG REFERENCE BOOKS

A Lectionary.

The basic book for liturgical planning. Every member of your committee needs to be familiar with the Sunday and daily lectionary—how it's set up, how the cycles work, what the different translations are like. If you're a chairperson and feeling mischievous, work up a quick lectionary quiz for your committee—you'd be justified in requiring them to pass it.

The big red parish lectionary shouldn't be locked up in the sacristy—there should be one or more copies available for borrowing and reference by your liturgy committee. For home use, there are several handy substitutes available. *Celebrating Liturgy* gives you all the Sunday readings (New American Bible translation) in a useful workbook format, along with some forgettable commentary. In a smaller size, the readings are available in *At Home with the Word*. The books are cheap and issued annually. Write Liturgy Training Publications, 155 East Superior Street, Chicago 60611.

(For a very brief historical look at how the lectionary got to be organized the way it is, you could look at *The Word in Worship* by William Skudlarek [Nashville: Abingdon, 1981], pp. 11-44. And for an outstanding basic series of commentaries on all three series of Sunday readings, there is Reginald H. Fuller's *Preaching the New Lectionary* [Collegeville: The Liturgical Press, 1974].)

A Sacramentary.

Less readable than the lectionary by far, this other big red book will acquaint you with all the presider's prayers for every Sunday, weekday, and feast. For home study of the eucharistic texts and prayers, buy a small paperbound Sunday missal; there are several to choose from. For a handy compendium of the basic texts and instructions for weddings, baptisms, confirmation, and funerals, committee members can get *The Rites* (New York: Pueblo, 1983).

There are several other references in the area of rites and texts that some of your committee members may want to become familiar with. *The Liturgy of the Hours* is available in both a complete four-volume set and several different one-volume abbreviations. Discovering the range and quiet beauty of the church's tradition of daily non-eucharistic prayer may wean you from the opinion that Sunday mass was ever a liturgy intended for private meditation. In addition, morning and evening prayer are often used successfully in a parish setting, and they can be an interesting alternative or supplement to a schedule of daily eucharists.

The more adventurous can also get a copy of *The Book of Common Prayer* (New York: Seabury, 1977). This isn't just a gesture towards ecumenism, although we trust you will be struck by the similarities between the rites in that book and the Roman sacramentary. The BCP is in its own right a fascinating source of liturgical prayers. Don't tell anyone where you stole them from.

THE LAW

All you really need to know in the way of official liturgical norms can be found in a small number of Vatican II and post-Vatican II documents. *The Constitution on the Sacred Liturgy* (1963, Vatican II), *The General Instruction of the Roman Missal* (tr. 1982), *Directory for Masses With Children* (1973), and the *Lectionary for Mass: Introduction* (1981) will provide you with the guidelines established by Rome for liturgical celebration.

For further norms established for the American church (and for your own enjoyment and inspiration) read the three outstanding documents from the American bishops: *Music In Catholic Worship* (1972, revised 1983), *Environment and Art in Catholic Worship* (1978) and *Liturgical Music Today* (1982).

All these documents (and others besides) are collected in the convenient and affordable *The Liturgy Documents: A Parish Resource*, published by Liturgy Training Publications in Chicago (see address under "A Lectionary" above). Make sure you get the revised (1985) edition. The documents are also available separately from the Office of Publishing Services, United States Catholic Conference, 1312 Massachusetts Avenue, NW, Washington, D.C. 20005.

FOR IDEAS AND INSPIRATION

Eugene A. Walsh, S.S., *The Theology of Celebration* (Old Hickory, Tennessee: Pastoral Arts Associates, 1977).
Eugene A. Walsh, S.S., *The Ministry of the Celebrating Community* (Old Hickory, Tennessee: Pastoral Arts Associates, 1977).
Eugene A. Walsh, S.S., *Practical Suggestions for Celebrating Sunday Mass* (Old Hickory, Tennessee: Pastoral Arts Associates, 1978).

Written in wonderfully plain English, these three small books are almost a liturgical library unto themselves. The first two establish a strong theology of eucharist as, primarily, celebration. The third is perhaps the most useful and realistic list of suggestions for improving weekly liturgies ever put between two covers. Even if you don't agree with everything Walsh suggests, there's no doubt that he's drawn a bead on the boredom and lethargy that permeate most of our "celebrations."

Tad Guzie, *The Book of Sacramental Basics* (New York: Paulist, 1981).
Tad Guzie, *Jesus and the Eucharist* (New York: Paulist, 1974).

The first book is as clear an explication as there is of the theology of celebration that links all the sacraments. Symbols, stories, baptism, marriage, confirmation, sacraments for children, and even the Rite of Christian Initiation of Adults—they're all your committee's business, and this is a thought-provoking but friendly book about how they work. The second (actually earlier) book is a more advanced treatment of eucharistic theology—even transsubstantiation and all that. Yet it's readable and fascinating, and will definitely make you think differently about what's going on at Sunday liturgy.

Joseph Gelineau, *The Liturgy Today and Tomorrow* (New York: Paulist, 1978).
Aidan Kavanagh, *Elements of Rite: A Handbook of Liturgical Style* (New York: Pueblo, 1982).

Gelineau—composer of the now omnipresent psalm settings—writes convincingly about congregation size, music, verbal overkill, and lots else. (While his book just recently went out of print, some bookstores and libraries should still have copies.) Kavanagh is unpredictable. In a gracefully written book overtly modelled after Strunk and White's *Elements of Style*, he provides a variety of perceptive and opinionated rules, principles, laws, suggestions, and even a list of common mistakes. You also get an excellent bibliography.

PERIODICALS (ONLY TWO)

Pastoral Music is the best magazine on liturgy now going,[1] and your committee (and probably all your members individually) ought to get a subscription. Its name is a bit misleading—you'll get feature articles and reviews not just about music but about all sorts of liturgy-related topics, most with a practical emphasis. *PM* is also a good way to keep up with conferences, workshops, new books and records, and liturgists and musicians looking for employment. *Pastoral Music* is included with membership in the National Association of Pastoral Musicians (which your parish also ought to get), but individuals can get the magazine separately. Write NPM, 225 Sheridan Street, N.W., Washington, DC 20011.

The other liturgy periodical you should be aware of is *Worship*, a handsome scholarly journal for those who want to take the study of liturgy more academically and historically. *Worship* combines excellent articles on current liturgical trends with arcane researches into such topics as the origin of matins. While you may not become a regular reader, you should at least know about *Worship*—it has played a major role in America's liturgical renewal. Write The Liturgical Press, Collegeville, Minnesota 56321.

1. This recommendation has not been influenced by the fact that the publisher of *Pastoral Music* is also the publisher of our book. (If you knew what they paid us for the book, you wouldn't even *suspect* us of a conflict of interest.)